KEZAR STADIUM
49ers Fans Remember

Martin S. Jacobs

Editing and Layout by Bob Zingmark
Photos from contributors and author's collection

ISBN: 9798681467540

First Printing: 2021

Independently published in U.S.A.

Authored by:

Martin S. Jacobs
P.O. Box 22026
San Francisco, CA 94122

To 49ers fans who graciously shared their memories
of Kezar Stadium, and helped make this book possible.

Table of Contents

Preface

Toward the end of the 19th, and beginning of the 20th Centuries, the growing sport of football was a good match for San Francisco - a punishing and inspiring contest for a cold, gritty and working-class city. It was a casual pastime for several years before football seemed to rise overnight into a local phenomenon. Organized teams appeared charging entry fees, and friendly exhibitions among Bay Area schools turned into full-blown rivalries. It's popularity grew, as spectators seemed thrilled and titillated by the game's action and violence.

In 1920, Jack Spaulding, an Olympic Club gridder, proposed an athletic stadium for San Francisco. Many city business leaders backed him, as it would put San Francisco on level with other cities having large stadiums. Two years later, the San Francisco Park Commission accepted a $100,000 gift from the estate of Mary A. Kezar, to build a memorial - Kezar Stadium - in honor of her mother and uncles, who were pioneers in the area. After the City and County of San Francisco appropriated an additional $200,000, the stadium was built in a year.

Kezar Stadium was constructed on the site of the old nursery and stable yard at the southeast corner of Golden Gate Park. Also on the site was John McLaren's beloved Rhododendron Dell. The stadium was laid out east-to-west, an unconventional layout for football, and a classic bowl shape made of concrete - mostly 60 rows deep and with a seating capacity of 59,000. In addition, a six-lane dirt track was installed, circling the stadium between the stands and field. Dedication ceremonies took place May 2, 1925, and featured a two-mile footrace between Ville Ritola and Paavo Nurmi, two celebrated Olympians from Finland. A little over a month later, Kezar Stadium hosted the USA Outdoor Track & Field Championships.

Professional football arrived in California in 1940, with the formation of the Pacific Coast Pro Football League (PCPFL), composed of five teams. At the time the National Football League (NFL) did not extend further west from Chicago. In 1942, a minor league team, the San Francisco Bay Packers joined the PCPFL. Like the other clubs, the Packers' roster was full of policemen, laborers, teachers and firefighters. They used Kezar as their home field.

World War II saw many professional athletes in all sports called to serve their country. The new league pressed on with a limited schedule. In 1944, the American Football League (AFL) formed with eight teams, and the San Francisco Clippers were born - also playing home games at Kezar. The two leagues competed with one another for the attention of fans throughout California, and ultimately decided the best course of action was to merge for the 1945 season.

In 1946, the newly franchised San Francisco 49ers, part of the All-American Football Conference (AAFC) was established. With larger crowds than the previously-named leagues, the 49ers had a foothold on the public's attention, and their desire for professional football featuring quality players. Two years later, due to dwindling interest, the PCPFL closed its doors.

On the 49ers opening day, August 20, 1946, the Golden Gate Bridge and Bay Bridge were filled with vehicles carrying fans to Kezar from as far away as 200 miles. It seemed like a ready-made box office attraction, but for the first game, Kezar was just a little over half-full. The 34-14 win over the Chicago Rockets merited just three paragraphs in the *San Francisco Chronicle* newspaper the following day, with horse racing taking-up an entire page.

The AAFC struggled, yet the 49ers grew into a success story under the coaching leadership of Buck Shaw, and star players, including quarterback Frankie Albert, and running backs John Strzykalski, Len Eshmont and Joe Perry. In 1950, after a string of winning seasons, the team survived the League's shutting down, and was welcomed into the National Football League, along with the Cleveland Browns and Baltimore Colts.

An emerging member of the NFL, the 49ers brought in a new generation of star players, including Y.A. Tittle, Hugh McElhenny, Leo Nomellini and Bob St. Clair - all eventual NFL Hall of Famers. Bob St. Clair played every one of his high school (Polytechnic), college (University of San Francisco) and professional (49ers) home games in Kezar, arguably the only person ever to do this in the same stadium.

Kezar Stadium was a star in its own right with many fans strolling the paths through Golden Gate Park to watch the 49ers play. For years the Christopher Milk section provided a free opportunity for young 49ers fans to attend games and win autographed footballs. Weather during the early Fall games was especially pleasant. Yet, on a clear day the glare of the sun settling above the west rim of the stadium would drive the players crazy. By the fourth quarter, the cold bite of the Pacific Ocean fog would cut through. The cold weather became the ultimate fans' stimulant. They passionately and steadfastly, took great pride in their 49ers. Outside of the "boo birds" and unruly drunks, they were considered to be the most amiable in the league.

Many 49ers fans felt it was a jinx the team never won an NFL championship, while playing at Kezar. The team did come close, however. In 1957, the 49ers made the Western Conference finals, and hosted a playoff game at Kezar vs the Detroit Lions. The winner of the game would play the Cleveland Browns for the NFL Championship the following weekend. The 49ers jumped into the lead for a good half of the game, yet the Lions rebounded and defeated them in a heart breaker, 31-27. A little over a decade later in 1970, before moving to a football renovated Candlestick Park, the 49ers made the playoffs, losing their final game played at Kezar vs the Dallas Cowboys, January 3, 1971.

Kezar Stadium remained a fixture and venue for local sports and concerts before it was demolished and rebuilt with a smaller seating capacity in 1989 - still called Kezar. In 2003, Kezar's field was dedicated and named in honor of Bob St. Clair.

Bob St. Clair holds plaque dedicating Kezar's field in his honor.
From left: Y.A. Tittle, St. Clair, Charlie Krueger, Joe Perry and Dan Colchico.

Forward

Kezar Stadium-49ers Fans Remember is a book written for every fan by fans from my generation who attended games at Kezar, listened to play-by-play radio and watched live televised broadcasts. After years of deliberation, I decided to rekindle the spirit of grand old Kezar and its pro football history, by authoring this book.

I reached out to the team owners and staff, players and coaches, broadcasters and journalists - all who witnessed memorable moments during the 49ers twenty-five year tenure at Kezar. I asked them for their most intriguing, maybe outlandish, heartfelt moments witnessing a game, and experiencing the stadium. The response was overwhelming.

Appropriate stories were selected to include in my book. Certain submissions were carefully modified at editor's discretion. Tone and spontaneity of provided Kezar memories and experiences remain intact.

I spent six-months converting facts and submissions into a manuscript, and shaping the material into an exciting, unfolding drama of the 49ers, and their attachment to Kezar. In addition I selected amazing, historic photographs from team photographers and fans, local newspaper archives and from my personal collection. This book is truly a 49ers fan's treasure to be preserved for future generations.

-Author

Introduction

At nine years old, I barely knew a forward pass from a lateral. My dad took me to my first 49ers football game. Now life would forever change.

We arrived early at Kezar Stadium on an August, 1952 Sunday. Nestled among giant oak trees at Golden Gate Park's southeastern end, the stadium looked like a huge toilet bowl. Overcast temps of about 60° was typical weather in the Cole Valley District. I was awestruck. In a long line we stood for two 50-cent end zone tickets. All around were 49ers fans in overcoats or leather jackets - some with beanie hats, and some drinking beer.

An exhibition game against the Chicago Cardinals was set. Inside the 25-cent program, I saw great photos of 49ers players in action poses. Then came a cartoon of a gold miner shooting two pistols, one aimed at his head! Dad said he was from the "gold rush" days. I fell in love with the little prospector.

Elation inside Kezar grew into a crescendo of boisterous fans. We climbed concrete stairs for good seats with a vantage point. Here before us was the full beauty of Kezar's field - bright green grass, thick white yard lines and towering goal posts. It took my breath away.

Roars from this crowd and blaring foghorns swallowed introductions of the 49ers players, one after another over a loud speaker.

"Good afternoon ladies and gentlemen ... this is Dave Scofield, your 49ers game announcer. Welcome to Kezar Stadium for today's game between the San Francisco 49ers, and the visiting Chicago Cardinals. And now, the starting lineups ..."

Before kickoff an armed forces color guard preceded by 49ers majorettes and marching band clad in spanking red and gold outfits came onto the field. After the National Anthem was played, they all marched toward the west end zone.

The players' names were unique. Had anyone heard of Y. A. Tittle - ever? Or Bob St. Clair? Hugh McElhenny? What a perfect name for a football player - "Mac-el-henny" - a name like no other. Magic was in their numbers too. No. 39 was McElhenny; No. 34 was Joe Perry; No. 14 was Tittle; No. 73 was Leo Nomellini. Dad told me Bob St. Clair could be identified without a number. You could tell him from other players by his height. At 6-feet 9-inches, he was the tallest player in the game.

When the game started, I was more interested in watching the 49ers mascot - a mule named "Clementine" parade around the stadium. I still remember the aroma of popcorn in the air, and the ice cream vendors chanting "yummy, yummy, good for the tummy."

Then a barrage of seagulls would swoop down, picking-up hot dog wrappers and paper cups off the wooden benches. I recall one seagull swipe the hot dog right from a fan's bun. It flew off, while I laughed hysterically. Dad said the gulls were well-trained to drop their castings on visitor's heads. Of course, dad was being facetious.

My first thoughts of football were: Why were all these guys running circles in different directions, and knocking one another down? People were yelling and booing it seemed after every play. Some were arguing with each other. Two men sitting nearby spent time drinking and screaming obscenities.

Halfway through the game, dad bought me a hot dog and soda. After awhile, I was asking dad to take us home. I buried my face against his shoulder. Still I remember the feel of his wool overcoat against my nose. He kept telling me to be patient. But, this boring game made no sense to me. Surely I could be having more fun with friends than this. Then what happened next, changed my life forever.

It was during the 3rd quarter when dad told me to watch number 39. From where we sat in the end zone behind the goal posts, number 39 was an ant. When dad handed me his binoculars, and I focused on number 39, something dynamic happened.

He got the ball on a pitch, cut wide to his right and headed-up the sidelines toward the west end. He then cut to the center of the field, swerving directly away from two defenders, yet head-on toward two more. I watched his every move. Would-be tacklers aimed at his long legs, hut he suddenly stopped, then immediately started in a new direction. Evading all defenders, he scored a touchdown without a single player touching him. All I could think about was "wow." A big crowd roar from the crowd broke my concentration. What a spectacular run! This guy was really fun to watch. Dad said his name was Hugh McElhenny, and this was his first game.

The 49ers won the game 38-14, but it didn't really matter. From then on, it was a time when mortality and immortality were so close. I had dreams almost every night of being a member of the 49ers. I could imagine the texture of a football in my hands, as Frankie Albert faded back to pass, or the elation of watching my favorite hero, McElhenny, catching a screen pass, and going all the way for a touchdown.

After a couple years, Kezar became my sanctuary. Each Sunday, I took special pride in being the first 49ers fan in the stadium, when the gates opened at 11:30 am. Like most kids, I was able to buy a 15-cent quart of Christopher Milk, and clip-out a coupon from the carton entitling me to free tickets to the games. The Christopher Milk section was located at the northeast corner of the stadium.

Actually the view was better than the end zone seats where my dad and I once sat. Kids were supposed to be 15-years old and under, but some fans looked old enough to be my uncle, drinking beer and smoking cigarettes. Obviously they weren't kids.

Each season, the 49ers opened their exhibition season in August. Grass looked so fresh, however, these conditions didn't last long. By mid-season there would only be dirt between the hash marks or 30-yard lines. By the 4th quarter of a game, foggy weather became the field's ultimate stimulant, and created lots of mud.

I later realized Kezar was a madhouse populated by passionate and brawling fans. It seemed that way especially during those waning years when the 49ers missed the playoffs. At the end of every season, the familiar chant was always "Wait 'til next year." And, we did.

Were the fans really that unruly? Not really - just frustrated. Fans' pride in the 49ers was unquestionable, and doubtless each fan was basically warm and sincere. Yet, I cannot imagine not looking up in the stands, and finding chaos on display. Never did I feel our fans needed a badge of loyalty to prove their mettle. Win or lose, they were just 49ers fans who cared about their team.

Looking back, I now have greater clarity for my team, and the stadium I loved. And though Kezar was a place where the cold bite of the Pacific Ocean fog would cut through my blood and chill my bones, it was a grand old stadium.

Of all great moments I've witnessed at Kezar, I'm glad for sticking around. Maybe it's because life is so full of repetition and tedium, while watching a game at Kezar was so melodramatic. For whatever reasons, it was worth it.

1

Pregame

"Fifty-three years ago in 1967, my sister Gwen and I drove up from Modesto for a Niners-Saints game. This would be our first time my sister and I attended a game at Kezar, but there was nowhere to park. Vehicles were lined up on Stanyan Street all the way up to Parnassus and surrounding streets, all looking for a place to park. We didn't expect the pregame experience to start with such insanity.

We had heard about the counterculture movement of the '60s in San Francisco, but we never realized what we were about to encounter. So, we ended up driving around for about an hour, until we found a parking space near a concourse in Golden Gate Park. We were told by some locals we had about a mile walk to the stadium. We also didn't realize on game days the park would be reveling with hippies. Many of them had long hair, donned in bright costumes, with garland beads and bracelets around their necks and wrists. There were sounds of distant bongos, tambourines and all kinds of acoustics, as we walked along towards the stadium.

We still had time to kill before the 1:30 p.m. kickoff. Once we reached Haight Street, we bought a few pretzels and sodas from a street vendor. As we got closer to the stadium, we saw a program seller on a corner. He had five bundles of programs on a dolly. We bought two of them at 50 cents each.

Once we reached Kezar, we realized the stadium was smack dab in a neighborhood surrounded by tall oak trees on one side and buildings on the other. People were cashing in on the proximity of the stadium by charging for parking in driveways. And, if you were not lucky enough to have tickets, the fans we saw on the rooftops of apartment buildings across the street from the stadium were watching the game for free.

In retrospect, the sights and sounds we witnessed that Sunday, long before the Niners and Saints took the field, remains a unique experience we will always cherish. And by the way, we enjoyed the game. The Niners beat the Saints 27-13 which made our day all the more worthwhile. I still have the program and ticket stub."

-Beth Chadwick

"I was at Kezar for their home opener against the Cardinals in 1957, as well as other games for the following 13 years. For this game I sat with the sporting press in the press box as a Kezar Stadium operations assistant, but had difficulty seeing the action on the field by the end of the first quarter. The second quarter it was still clear enough, but the first wispy trailers of fog began sneaking into the stadium.

During the game I was kept pretty busy, as there were no elevators in the press box, and often I delivered messages going down the steps, through the crowd, to down on the field, to the coaches. This went on throughout the game. By the time the third quarter started, the fog was whirling across the field. This was 49ers football in the fog, soon to become a tradition, like the cable cars and sourdough bread. We lost the game 20-10, against a team we were supposed to beat.

As time passed, I became the head of football operations at Kezar. That lasted nine years, and I had the responsibility seven days a week, and continued through the end of the game. I had to be sure the pre-game activity proceeded like clockwork. A week prior to a game, the visitors equipment manager would call me with the teams arrival, I'd check on hotel reservations, bus schedules, and equipment pickup from the airport, and any special needs for the game.

The officiating crew usually arrived on Saturdays for a walk-through of the stadium. Visiting teams preferred to arrive on Saturdays to get in an afternoon practice. They used the Kezar triangle, a grass area outside the west end of the stadium, Sharon Meadows, the Polo Grounds in Golden Gate Park, and City College of San Francisco.

The mornings of the game, our technicians would conduct a final inspection of the entire stadium, including the public address system, the lighting, the security and playing field, as well as halftime participants' routines and schedules.

During games, I also used a spotter in the press box who helped each team's medical staff spot potential injuries which might occur. Before warm-ups one of the locker room assistants presented the game balls to the officials for inspection. Wilson footballs were the choice of the NFL.

And lastly, before a game an emergency ambulance and paramedics had to be in place at the west end zone tunnel. I'd meet on the field with the officials and security personnel, and the SFPD to review procedures in case of an emergency during and after the games."

-Bruce Ledger

"I remember before our two-mile walk from our home on Lincoln Way to Kezar Stadium, we'd make our pit stop at the Shamrock, a homey Irish pub anchored in nostalgia for old 49ers fans. We made it a cultural hangout. I remember once the electricity went out, and they lit candles and kept pouring drinks. Tavahn Ghazi, the historic bar owner, served us stromboli and to-go drinks. We were pretty well toasted by the time we got to the stadium."

-Shea Shawnson

"I'm almost 69, and I grew-up in South San Francisco. My story about Kezar is actually about the last game played there between the 49ers and Cowboys. My cousin Don and I camped out at the stadium the night before in line for 5,000 general admission tickets to go on sale. Being the kind of guy I was back then, I figured we needed a lot of beer. Don picked me up some beer right after dinner. I grabbed my sleeping bag and a blanket and put on my heavy jacket and off we went.

When we got there, we were able to park in the main lot. There were probably only about ten people in line, maybe more. But, I remember we were close to the front. We were told no more than four tickets per person was allowed, but we were so broke, all we had was barely enough for two. We took our place in line and started to hang out. Someone had a football we were all tossing around. I always pretended I was John Brodie or Gene Washington. The 49ers were so good back then. Their defense was great and the offense could really move the ball.

Eventually, it was time to pass out, and we were all in our place in line in our sleeping bags. The next morning we probably woke-up around 7:00 a.m. When I looked back, the line was a mile long. But, in the next couple of hours the crowd grew to a couple thousand, and it started to get uneasy. People were pressing forward. When finally the ticket booth windows opened, the line behind us disintegrated, as people from the back rushed to the front. We went from about tenth in line to probably 50th. We tried constantly to keep our place with strong elbowing of people behind us. Finally, we got up to the ticket booth, and got our two end zone tickets. I laugh at that, because scalping just wasn't the thing back then, and besides we were broke.

So guess what? I got sick, got a fever, and felt like crap. But, Don suggested I get some blackberry brandy, and we headed out back to Kezar. I felt better. We were pumped-up, because it was our last game ever at Kezar, and always a huge game against those hated Cowboys.

We got to our seats, but were far down the aisle - very low and near the corner. Well, we lost the game, but the brandy did the trick. The winning touchdown by the Cowboys receiver was right in front of me.

That catch is ingrained in my mind for eternity. Kezar was such a part of my life back then, and I wouldn't change those early years for anything."

-Fred Cesano

"I worked at Kezar during high school, 1967-71. My father taught at Polytechnic High School, across the street from the stadium. He knew the Kezar Pavilion superintendent, Ed Blount. Ed would ask the visiting team if they needed help on the field, and often I helped him. I would get to the stadium around 10:00 a.m. to see if I was going to work, and if not, I would sit in the Christopher Milk section. While waiting outside the locker rooms, I noticed Charlie Krueger pull-up. He was always the first one there, and drove a red Ford pickup. He'd get out of his truck wearing his Levi's and cowboy boots. He was a very personable guy.

Under the guidance of their equipment manager, my job was laying out the visitors' equipment and supplies, like hanging their jerseys, and putting rolls of tape in each stall. Sometimes I would carry the equipment bags, rain gear, capes and jackets, coolers that held the Gatorade and water bottles to the field, making five or six trips through the tunnel. It was also my job to provide a dozen primary, and a dozen back-up footballs to the officials. The equipment manager usually gave me $10 for the day, and maybe a couple of t-shirts. I do remember getting paid by Bears coach George Halas - $10, all in one-dollar bills.

During that particular game it was raining, and one of the 49ers was hurt on the Bears sideline. One Bears players told the medical crew to bury him right there! I heard a lot of outrageous comments, and did see lots of fights in the stands and on the field. Wow, I'm just realizing that was 50 years ago.

Walking out of the tunnel and onto the field with the visiting players for warm-ups was an experience, and they were usually very loud. After games, the top of the cyclone fence above the entrance to the tunnel was covered in beer cups or bottles. Once during halftime, I had to go back to the locker room, and was shocked to see players smoking cigarettes, while in their uniforms - the Cowboys Bob Lilly, Charlie Waters, and Dan Reeves to name a few.

After we lost to Dallas in the championship game, I was given a football from the equipment manager. That day Duane Thomas and Calvin Hill ran all over the 49ers. After the game I got all their autographs."

-Patrick Ebert

"For two seasons (1968-69), we had season tickets on the North side of Kezar, but always opted for the West end zone. I was 14 at the time. We could stretch out, and our section was always filled with interesting characters. I remember the color guard came out for the pregame activities, all in full uniforms with chrome plated helmets. When completed, they would exit into a tunnel near us at the West end of the stadium.

Some ant-war idiot felt it would be a good idea to hurl a beer bottle at them. It hit one of the honor guard holding the flag square in the helmet, and dropped him to the ground. Some fans two rows up from us rushed the hurler and roughed him up pretty good, sending him cascading down the cement steps. There was a standing ovation for the 'patriots.'

Every game was an adventure for us in that end zone. Usually, drunk fans threw cushions after a bad loss, yet still it made us fans forever."

-Tom Monahan

"A teaching career brought me to the San Francisco Bay Area, where I immediately established allegiance to the Niners. I approached this challenging lifestyle from two fronts: first was my creation of my 'Niners Fan Van' to transport other fans to Kezar Stadium. This eventually gave way to a 24-seat school bus painted in Niners colors with a banner: '49ers Boosters'. On game days, I was able to park my bus behind the band concourse in Golden Gate Park, about a mile from Kezar. The unique feature of my bus included a police siren, a fog horn, a 3,000 watt sound system and a banjo.

Secondly, based on standards established by my uncle Willard, I took fan enthusiasm to a new level, and began to transform my appearance to show my identity and loyalty to the team, by wearing a red ball cap, a Pendleton shirt resembling a gold miner, and a red cape with "49ers" screened on the back. Eventually, our group became known as the '49ers Booster Club of Santa Clara'."

-Tom Bragalone

"My parents purchased their season tickets the month I was born in 1946. They were the 523rd people to buy 49ers season tickets. They loved, lived and breathed 49ers football at Kezar. In the beginning, those going to the games consisted of my father, mother, and grandfather. Some years later, if my parents were unable to attend games, they gave their tickets to friends. The only catch was they had to bring me with them. Later, my sister and I used my parents' tickets.

Before games, we made it a ritual to find an area to tailgate in

Golden Gate Park, where fans would congregate before games, and we'd look for ones to mingle with. One of my favorite landing spots was right behind the Children's Playground next to a big grass meadow, just across the street from the stadium. We'd get their early, so we could ride the merry-go-round, and buy a 15-cent hot dog and some pink popcorn. It made our day. Then we'd run over to Kezar for the 1:30 p.m. kickoff."

-John and Betty Rezonya

"We used to sit on the front porch of our flat on Clayton Street and listen to 49ers games with Lon Simmons. It was common to hear... 'Tittle back to pass, he looks, he throws ....' We were lucky enough and young enough to rent parking spaces in front of our driveway and earn a few bucks. Kezar had a paucity of parking to say the least. In later years, I could afford a season ticket, and watch the games in person. I would bring my transistor radio with me just to listen to Simmons broadcast the games."

-Ken Kelly

"As a kid in the '50s, it was easy to sneak into a game at Kezar. Around 9:00 a.m., I would go to the North entrance next to the police station. Gate 10 to be exact. The vendors were unloading their trucks. I would help them, and on the third trip I would just stay inside the corridor until the game started. I always found a good seat."

-D. Wilkens

"My dad and grandfather lived on Frederick Street in 1950 and '51. Their building could provide parking for four or five cars in the garage. They would sell those spaces on game day for $3 apiece, and made enough money each game to take our whole family - all four of us - to Kezar on the $12 they made in parking fees."

-Michael Tokmakoff

"I played Pop Warner football in 1952, for the Les Vogel Chevrolet Power Gliders. We practiced at the Panhandle, and played our home games at Kezar Stadium. Before one 49ers game, we entertained the crowd for a 15-minute exhibition game. What a thrill that was, except I fumbled the ball on my only carry for a two-yard loss. Still, we got to use the 49ers dressing room at the time the 49ers players headed towards the tunnel to the playing field - another thrill being so close to them."

-Byron Nelson

"I remember my dad took me to several games at Kezar in the 1950s. We always tried to make it to the Chicago Bears games. As we entered Kezar, I had on a new quilted jacket I got for my birthday, and a seagull crapped on it. This guy behind us said: 'Sonny, I don't think it's going to be a great day for you'. Needless to say, those were the days when George Blanda actually played quarterback for the Bears. That dynamite hookup he had with Harlon Hill was fabulous."

-Bob Greenberg

"My father, uncle, and I used to walk to Kezar from where we lived at 23rd Avenue, between Irving Street and Lincoln Way. As a little girl, I thought it was like walking a hundred miles to the stadium, even though I walked every school day to St. Anne's school on Funston. In my mind, the two places were much farther apart than they actually were."

-Judy Fiore

"On Saturday evenings, when the 49ers played at Kezar the following day, I would drive my parents car to the stadium to stake out a good parking space for them, and leave the car. I had a friend follow me and bring me back. The next morning, the day of the game, my parents took the 72 bus to the stadium to see the game. After the game, they would retrieve their well-placed and conveniently parked car, and drive home. This was the way of a wily native San Franciscan."

-Vicky Carfagni Berol

"We have many good memories of Kezar. My older brother and I sold programs there. It was quite an adventure for a twelve or thirteen-year old kid. I could only carry 50 programs at a time, but I made a few bucks. I remember watching the TV crew working on Frederick Street reporting scores from other NFL games, and watching John Brodie warming up with Gene Washington on the sidelines. I also met Lon Simmons, the 49ers broadcaster. He was a great man."

-M. Lingua

"When the Niners practiced at the Polo Fields in Golden Gate Park, I nearly got included in a team picture. I was in the 5th or 6th grade at the time, and a couple of players thought it would be funny to have me in the team picture, while others didn't. I got bounced from the photo."

-Patrick Koneen

"Between the ages of 10 and 13, I sold programs at Kezar. I was from the Sunset District, an easy bike ride through the Park to the Children's Playground, where I parked my bike. I sold my programs on Stanyan Street. Not only could I earn about $10 for a few hours work, but the best part was a free pass to the game and to find an empty seat. And, there were quite a few in those days. I have great memories of the time."

-Gary Goddard

"My dad owned Mulready's Dry Goods on the corner of Haight and Ashbury. We would walk Haight to Stanyan, then over to Kezar. Dad would stop at bars for a drink, and a cafe to eat Swedish meatballs before the games. I don't know why the memory sticks in my mind.

My other memory is being at the North end of the stadium parking lot, standing by the railing, and looking down, as players left their dressing rooms. Seeing Brodie, Parks, Nomellini and others up-close was so exciting. I remember stories from my dad of fights and broken windows in the neighborhood after losing to Detroit in the playoffs."

-Danny Baptista

"Going to Kezar in the late '60s was kind of a weird place to watch a football game. First, there was absolutely no parking, so we'd drive around Golden Gate Park, and then the Haight looking for a spot. Once we found someplace to park, which was usually in someone's driveway, we walked down Haight Street, which was overflowing with hippies. It was a strange scene. There were young kids sitting around the street smoking pot and looking for handouts. People would try to sell us drugs as we walked to the stadium. I guess we looked like we had money, because we carried a cooler with beer and dressed well. These kids were in another world, and it was like they were oblivious to the fact that 60,000 people were gathering for a football game a few blocks away."

-Julie Miles

"My dad and his boss went to a Niners game at Kezar in 1960. While looking for a parking space, they found a young Chinese boy sitting on a driveway reading the Sunday funnies. He told my dad's boss his parents said to rent the spot for $10. It was only three blocks from the stadium on 2nd Ave. So we jumped on the parking space. After the game the car was not parked in the driveway. An elderly African American couple answered the door, and my dad actually asked them if they had a Chinese son? They slammed the door and locked it, as my dad stifled a laugh. Final toll: $10 to the enterprising kid who robbed my dad and stole his automobile. The following day my dad tried calling the 49ers office to explain what happened. But, to no avail they couldn't help."

-Dave Santori

2

The Stadium

"I was born in 1976, in Mexico City. You may ask how was a kid from south of the border so engaged with current 49ers, then fall in love with the old-timers from Kezar Stadium? It began when I was watching the NFC Championship game against the Cowboys ('The Catch') on TV with my father, when I asked him a crucial question: 'Why do you like football so much?' His answer was epic, and marked the beginning of my great 'fandom'. 'Can't you see I'm the owner of that team?' I asked, 'how come?' He said: 'look at the letters on their helmets, those are my initials: 'SF' for Silverio Fernandez'. For a couple of years, I really thought my father was the owner of the 49ers. From then on, my love for the team increased yearly, and the championships really helped.

How was this related with Kezar? I really wanted to know about the heroes who made this franchise possible before Mr. Eddie D. It took me on a huge, fascinating tour of our team's past, which really has been amazing. Martin Jacobs book, *49ers Legends*, has been very informative in discovering our team's history.

Our first owner (which I learned at seven-years old wasn't my father), Tony Morabito, a well-deserving finalist for the Pro Football Hall of Fame in 1973, is one of my memorabilia obsessions. His autograph was really tough to get. He died on October 27, 1957, during a football game against the Chicago Bears at Kezar. After years looking, I was able to get his autograph directly from Canton.

I learned about Kezar Stadium in the late '90s. All I knew at the time was Candlestick Park, and was able to attend my first 49ers game in 1994 - the last year we won a Super Bowl at the 'Stick.' Once I got deep into the history of our team, I read about Kezar, and thought it might have met the same fate as our uncomfortable - but beloved Candlestick Park. To my surprise, Kezar was reconstructed, and renovated with a 10,000 seating capacity.

On February 2016, I started a journey to finally visit the place where it all began, and what a journey. I went from my hotel near Fisherman's Wharf to Golden Gate Park, and once there asked for directions. To my surprise, most people didn't knew what I was talking about, 'a stadium, here? No, I don't know' were constant answers So, 'please help me Google', and Eureka!

Finally, I was there, and it was awesome. Although it was renewed, I could feel the vibes of Frankie Albert, Alyn Beals, Leo Nomellini, and the whole 'Million Dollar Backfield' playing on the beautiful grass.

Here I was a young, old-time fan paying respect with a visit to where my passion started. While walking down the steps, I met another tourist who told me 'they should have taken the seagulls with them when they moved away.' It was hilarious. What else could they have brought from their previous home to honor their past? This is how my father's history lesson unchained a faithful journey to Kezar. I'm forever thankful for all the history I've learned."

-Cesar Fernandez Souza

"During the 1956 season, a member of the Board of Supervisors of the City and County of San Francisco criticized the manner in which Kezar Stadium was being operated. He was particularly critical of the concessions - cold hot dogs, uncleanliness and lack of adequate rest room facilities. His remarks inferring the 49ers were responsible for concessions and upkeep of stadium facilities, were carried in stories published in local papers. Nothing was further from the truth.

The truth was the 49ers had a lease agreement with the City and County of San Francisco to use Kezar for the sole purpose of presenting pro-football to the general public. The 49ers paid a rent based on paid attendance, and had no jurisdiction in the manner of concessions, cleanliness of comfort stations, or the stadium in general.

Operations, such as concession stands and vendors, were handled by Harry M. Stevens, America's foremost ballpark concessionaire based in New Jersey. The actual stadium operations from the janitorial services, playing field, scoreboards, and surroundings, were handled by the San Francisco Park and Recreation services."

-John Paul

"From 1950 to 1963, I ran a concession stand at Kezar during Niner games. It was a wonderful part-time job. My regular job was as a contractor. Our stand was located near the entrance to section KK. It was an exciting time, and the environment was great meeting all those Niner fans. Only drawback was missing the action on the field. I used three helpers in the booth, and paid them by the game - about $10. My workers usually were aged 16 to 18.

We had a catering company do the set-up for each game. By 9:00 a.m. they delivered containers of soda, cases of beer, packages of hot dogs, boxes of peanuts, trays of candy and cigarettes, along with the novelties and souvenirs. Then we started steaming hot dogs, brewing coffee around 10:00 a.m., and being ready to serve by 11:30 a.m., when the gates opened for the fans."

-Isadore Felzer

"As the Park Superintendent for Kezar Stadium, I performed periodic inspections weekly, making recommendations on needed repairs and installations to the management. Some of my duties included inspecting the structure of the stadium, both internally and externally, looking for any defects, cracks in walls, corrosion on the pipes, stadium lighting, and any minor defects around the facility. Electrical engineers and maintenance workers assisted me with the upkeep of the stadium."

-Julius Girod

"I was a police reserve officer for the SFPD, and worked security at Kezar during the '50s and '60s. I oversaw the playing field to deter theft, vandalism and unauthorized entry onto it. Before and after games, I greeted and directed traffic, as well as control access to the facility. The best part of the job was watching the games for free."

-Virgil Lombardi

"What do I remember about Kezar? When I was trying to get autographs during the 1955 season, a group of us kids and some adults, would gather early outside the players locker rooms. When the players arrived in their cars, they parked and walked to the clubhouse through the assemblage of autograph seekers.

My usual dodge was to sidle up to a player and say: 'Can I have your autograph?' Hugh McElhenny for example, took my program and opened it to an advertisement of himself holding Blue Seal Bread, and signed his name across it. The only player who ever gave me any trouble was Gordy Soltau. I spotted him talking to some fans, and went over and asked him for his autograph. 'I'm not Gordy Soltau!', he said. 'You have me confused with someone else'. Soltau was truly unique.

During slack times, we collectors would confer, exchanging inside information and dialogue. Near the end of the season, we compared notes. No one had a signature of John Henry Johnson. Y.A. Tittle or Joe Perry. But, by season's end - except for John Henry - I had them all.

At the last home game, I had a hunch and prowled among the cars in the parking lot. The front end of one car tilted. I looked through the window and saw John Henry Johnson asleep in the back seat. It was tempting to just leave him alone, but I decided to tap on the window. He opened one eye. John Henry didn't seem very happy to see me, but rolled the window down while lying flat on his back. I thought, what strong fingers.

'What do ya want?', he said to the effect. 'Can I have your autograph Mr. Johnson? It's the only one I don't have.' 'On one condition', he said. 'Promise me you won't tell anybody where I'm at.'

I promised, and didn't tell anybody until the following season. By then, the information was useless, because John Henry went to the Detroit Lions."

-R. Horton

"It was October 25, 1964. My friend Steve and I had a plan. We didn't have a ticket to the game against the Vikings at Kezar, but we heard from our friends, if we stood outside the stadium, sometimes fans would offer kids extra tickets. Well, it happened at least for this game, and the only time we tried it. We were just standing there, and then someone came up to us and asked us if we wanted two tickets. 'Sure', we said. The seats weren't bad. My memory has faded some, but

I think we were near the 40-yard line. I also think that day there were more seagulls than fans.

The game wasn't a classic by any means, as the teams traded scores back and forth. But, it did become noteworthy. Billy Kilmer, playing halfback, fumbled the ball. The Vikings Jim Marshall, a future Hall of Famer and one-fourth of the "Purple People Eaters", scooped-up the ball, and rumbled 66-yards, crossing our goal line. 31,000 fans went crazy! At first, I didn't have a clue what happened. Then Steve informed me Marshall ran the wrong way, and scored a safety for us. Niners center, Bruce Bosley, was the first to congratulate poor Marshall who couldn't believe it. He repeated a feat Roy Riegels from Cal did in the 1929 Rose Bowl.

The Vikings had the last laugh, as they won the game, and Marshall had vindicated himself. Later I read Mr. Riegels sent Marshall a letter that simply said, 'Welcome to the club'."

-Gordon Analla

"When I think of Kezar, our 49ers founder, Tony Morabito, comes to mind. If it hadn't been for Tony's intuition and tenacity bringing San Francisco its first major professional team, we would not have shared all of our Sunday's experiences - the 'alley-oops', the come-from-behind wins, and playoff games we endured at Kezar.

The Bay Area had been a mecca for college football. Tony saw the potential of professional football for our city, and presented his case in 1942, to National Football League officials, but was turned down. Tony didn't stop there. In Spring 1944, he took another crack, and filed an application for an expansion team to league commissioner, Elmer Layden. Again he was shunned. Not giving up, he was put in touch with Arch Ward, sports editor of *The Chicago Tribune*, who was trying to organize a rival league, the All-America Football Conference. Almost immediately, Tony told Arch to count him in. Tony agreed to form a San

Francisco franchise in a league that would begin operations in 1946. The rest is history. It only seems fitting that Tony Morabito be mentioned. I think all 49ers faithful will agree."

-Aaron Peskin

The Press Box

Here's a partial list of invitees to the Kezar Stadium press box for the Oct. 30,1960 game (49ers-Chicago Bears). It includes team management, broadcasters, newspaper journalists, 49ers players' family members, and VIP guests. The press box held 200 holding passes. List was supplied by Dave Boronio, *Vallejo Times-Herald*.

Bob Fouts- TV play-by-play announcer
Lon Simmons, Bob Blum, Gordy Soltau, Station KSFO
Art Rosenbaum, Bill Leiser, *San Francisco Chronicle*
Bob Brachman, Prescott Sullivan, *San Francisco Examiner*
Walt Daley, Jack McDonald, *News-Call Bulletin*
Cooper Rollow, *Chicago Daily Tribune*
Alan Ward, *Oakland Tribune*
Ira Blue, Station KGO, San Francisco
Hal Wolf, Station KNBC, San Francisco
Dick Templeton, *Redwood City Tribune*
Jack Bluth, *San Mateo Times*
Bill Feist, *San Jose Mercury News*
Wilbur Adams, *Sacramento Bee*
Dan Galvin, Station KSRO, Santa Rosa
Ed Orman, *Fresno Bee*
Jack Connolly, *San Rafael Independent Journal*
John Baggerly, *Los Gatos Times*
Jim Roach, *Modesto Bee*
Jay Ross, *Petaluma Argus-Courier*
Jerry Gandy, *Contra Costa Gazette*
Dan Brodie, 49ers statistician
Vic and Josephine Morabito, co- owners
Franklin Mieuli, co-owner
Albert Ruffo, co-owner
James Ginella, co-owner
Lou Spadia, general manager
Lyn Waldorf, chief scout
Dan McGuire, publicity director
Nathan Seardigi, controller
George Christopher, mayor of San Francisco
Alfonso Zirpoli, San Francisco supervisor
Celebrities: Mort Sahl, Danny Kaye, Johnny Mathis,
Hoagy Carmichael, Les Crane and Robert Cummings

"If you had gone to a Niners game at Kezar, and headed to section T, row 24, seats 16-17-18, you would have found one - Joe Berliffe, and his two boys. We were known as the 'chain gang'. On every Niners first down, we turned and faced the crowd, and led a chant: 'Move those chains...move those chains!' When the team left for Candlestick, we were heartbroken. Kezar was our sanctuary. We loved the stadium and everything about it. We were there from the beginning, and almost immediately began our routine chant with a few other partners in crime. After the last game against Dallas, we gathered as many souvenirs as possible. My son Tom left the stadium with a wooden 'Reserved Seat' sign that hung over one of the entrances. I found another that read 'General Admission'. Because of our fanaticism for the Niners, our roles as fans can best be summed-up with how much we enjoyed cheering...booing....and chanting at the games."

-Joe Berliffe

"To me, Kezar Stadium was a shrine, much like Fenway Park, Wrigley Field, or the L A Coliseum. Kezar had an aura all it's own - nothing like it. During the '51 season, I traveled with the team's statistician to other NFL stadiums, such as Soldier Field and Connie Mack Stadium, but none of those had the beauty of Kezar. The intensity of our fans was unmatched. Somehow our stadium mirrored the image of the team and our great city. Our fans were so passionate with reveled, unapologetic devotion, and tradition to timelessness. If you had asked any NFL player from that era which stadium he preferred playing-in, most likely Kezar would be at the top of his list."

-Philip Hopper

"Across the street from Kezar was Poly High. I hated P. E. class, as we had to run the perimeter track at Kezar everyday. Because of tradition and a bit of superstition, every high school football game we played at Kezar, coach Milt Axt had us enter the stadium at street level, and descend the same steps to the track. I thought it would have been an interesting article in one of the newspapers to highlight the connection between our coach Axt, two of his players, the Niners and Kezar. I don't know any other school having three of it's football players play on the same stadium field, while in high school and professionally. We did. They were Bob St. Clair, Alyn Beals and Gary Lewis. All played at Kezar, and all played for the 49ers. Milt Axt was also a scout for the Niners, and George Seifert, who also played football for Poly, became head coach with the 49ers. Poly had a lot of heritage."

-Mike Cassetta

"We all have a certain perspective of what Kezar Stadium means to us. My viewpoint is not as a player on the field, a coach on the side-lines, or fan in the bleachers. My perspective is from the hospital, University of California (UCSF), up the street from the stadium. As I looked down at Kezar, a huge boost of hope ran within me. Kezar was reminding me of days when I was a 49ers cheerleader. Kezar was telling me no matter what happens, I'll be okay. Kezar was what my heart needed at a time when there was a haze and fog overcoming me.

Memories of Kezar are woven together with memories of years of struggle. The wins and losses in life, perhaps are the most important lessons I learned, while I stood on the eighth floor looking at Kezar. Keep going, do not ever give up, and lean on those who will stand on the sidelines with you through the wins and losses.

Kezar is my ray of sunshine. It captures hope and represents an important era of our 49ers legacy. Cheers to the team and Kezar, for adding a little red and gold into our lives. The sight of the stadium makes us smile, and our decades-long 49ers memories live on in our hearts."

-Jeannie Liao

"My grade school was Neil Cummins in Corte Madera. Two of our teachers, avid sport fans, made it possible for some of us to attend a few professional sports games at Kezar. A special section for schools was sponsored by Christopher Milk who offered tickets at a reduced rate to schools.

On October 25, 1964, we attended the game between the Vikings and the 49ers. Jim Marshall of the Vikings recovered a fumble, and ran the wrong direction, resulting in a 49ers safety. The game ball was given to one of the kids in our section. You can imagine what a thrill it was, considering what Marshall had done - even though he was from the opposing team. After the game, players mingled among us on the field. We secured autographs from players willing to give them, and I was one of the lucky ones to get a chinstrap from one of the players. I still cherish that memento to this day.

Both my parents attended Poly High, and lived in the area after they married. My dad was on the Poly football team, and practiced and played his games at Kezar. It was unique, as Kezar was within walking distance from school. Over the years, dad talked about his experiences playing there. One comment I remembered in particular, was when he parked his car next to the stadium before a 49ers game, and his hubcaps were stolen. He complained to the 49ers management, but said nothing came of it."

-Linda Walsh Bruemmer

"Kezar Stadium was one of the most architecturally attractive stadiums in the whole country. It was an object of beauty, as well of utility. Thank you Willis Polk (the stadium's architect)."

- Herbert Fleishhacker

"When I worked at Kezar, we usually had a crew of eight to twelve gardeners who handled the equipment: rakes, hoes, mowers, and so forth. A few were responsible for the irrigation system, and made sure there were no protrusions on the grass field. We used an automatic irrigation watering system, which ran on an annual schedule. Kezar had natural grass, and in the off-season, we filled the pot holes with new grass, so there would be no soil exposed. We made sure the soil was well-drained with no standing water, although sometimes during foggy and wet weather in the Fall, we had numerous puddles. Also, we made sure there were no ruts or trenches caused by equipment use, no weeds with thorns, bristles or burrs, or holes made by moles and gophers, and other animals, which occasionally showed.

Usually on Thursday mornings during the season, as high schools played in the afternoon, we used a water-based paint for the yard lines and hash marks, without impeding the elongation of the grass blades. One of the workers would use a wheelbarrow called 'stripers' to make the lines. We repeated this on Saturdays before the Sunday 49ers games. On Mondays, a clean-up crew would come in, and remove all debris from the stadium."

-Walter DeGennaro

"I don't think any person could have enjoyed anything in life as much as we enjoyed going to Kezar. In that time, my family wasn't wealthy, but we always seemed to find our way to see the Niners play. No one wore replica jerseys back then. Team merchandise was nearly nonexistent. We wore overcoats and wide brim hats, and made home-made signs. Here's the big one: with no computer devices yet invented, people made eye contact. We listened to Lon Simmons on our transistor radios. That's how it was in those days."

-Len Kravitz

"My brother and I would hustle at the end of the games to pickup Kezar seat cushions. We'd collect, between 30-40, and reap the 5-cent deposit paid on each one, then split the few dollars."

-Dan Cerri

"In 1956, at age nine, I started attending Niners games at Kezar. My grandfather went to the warm-weather games, and I got to go to the cold-weather games with dad. During the games I attended, dad would send me down at halftime for hot dogs, as the lines were forever long. It didn't matter to me, because I really didn't understand the game. But, at around age 13, I became hooked on the Niners.

I started getting part-time jobs in 1968, and eventually became a season ticket holder, until 1970, when the Niners moved away. Suddenly, my penchant for a Niners championship would be forgotten. My memories of Kezar are endless. Looking back, the best part of going to the games was interacting with the fans and players. I miss those days, and I still wear their team colors with the same enthusiasm I once did at the games."

-Joe Banowsky

"The East end of the stadium had an entry and exit for the players arriving and departing the field. There was fencing around it to prevent the disgruntled crowd from throwing bottles at players exiting at halftime, or game's end. It seemed everyone had a flask or cup of beer to keep their spirits up. This resulted in a beer shower for the players. Some fans would remove their Zippo lighters from their pockets, heat-up pennies, then drop them down through the fencing. At times the pennies would lodge into a player's shoulder pads. It was a horrific experience for some players."

-Jeff Blumb

Team Equipment

Flannigan & Nold were consigned by the San Francisco 49ers for moving football equipment for their organization, as well as the visiting team's to and from the airports to Kezar Stadium and it's training facilities. Below estimate is from 1950, submitted by Susie Flannigan.

May 15, 1950

Mr. Alvin N. "Bo" McMillian
Detroit Lions Football Assn.
1401 Michigan Avenue
Detroit 16, Michigan

Gentlemen:

Our organization has handled the transportation of football equipment of the visiting teams that have played the San Francisco 49ers here on the west coast for the past three years.

Once again the season approaches and we are circularising the teams that will be playing at Kezar Stadium in San Francisco this fall. In the past, we have handled the equipment for the Baltimore Colts, Cleveland Browns, Chicago Hornets, Harvard University and Michigan State University to mention a few.

Listed below are tentative costs subject to waiting charges of $2.20 per hour due to the possibility of late arrival of plane.

From Oakland Airport to Hearst Ranch, PLeasanton, California.. 25.00
From Hearst Ranch to Kezar Stadium, S.F.................................. 30.00
From Kezar Stadium to Pleasanton, Calif..................................... 30.00
or
From Kezar Stadium to Oakland Airport....................................... 25.00

$110.00

Should you desire to use our services, drop us a line giving arrival time, date and place. Please be assured our truck and two men will be ready and waiting your arrival.

Trusting we may hear from you, we are

Yours truly,

Louis F. Nold
Flannigan & Nold
161 College Ave
San Francisco, 12, Calif.

"In the '60s, my father had nine season tickets to games at Kezar. He would often bring as many as seven of his 11 children, to watch the 49ers play. To get to games, we usually walked down Haight Street from our home on Cole Street. The stadium was adjacent to the Haight Ashbury District. In 1967, there was probably no greater, side-by-side contrast of diverging trends in American culture, than between fans at the stadium watching a game on grass, and people on Haight Street smoking grass.

I followed the fate of the 49ers with passionate intensity. I did not care about the extraordinarily odd, and presumably transient hippies on the other side of the stadium wall. I assumed, the only way they could have a long term impact on my world was - if one of them ran over one of us with their Volkswagen bus. Once the game ended, we walked very gingerly back home."

- Eric Anderson

"Kezar was an unusual facility. All rows of seats were benches, and each seat only 17 inches apart. There was virtually no parking at Kezar - only 300 slots for 'official' use, which meant press, politicians, and friends of politicians. Still, Kezar had its charm. Because the best weather months in the city were September and October, the early season games at Kezar were especially pleasant. On the sunny side, young men often took off shirts to soak up the sun. Fans would picnic in the park before coming to a game. If you got to Kezar a couple of hours early, you could see people walking across the park. It was a very special scene. The smell of the freshly cut grass at Kezar in August, made me think of the fields of lawns in Golden Gate Park. The smell of steamed hot dogs on a steamed bun, and a bottle of beer still remind me of that grand old Kezar Stadium."

- Joe Kaplan

"I still don't know why the 49ers left Kezar for Candlestick. For whatever reason, I think of Candlestick as a baseball park. They should have never played football there. They should have just renovated Kezar. Maybe the 49ers would still be in San Francisco today."

- Fred Schneider

"Kezar is enshrined in my memory forever. The stadium had many historic moments. I saw Frankie Albert 'the T-formation wizard' make his first pass, and run for a touchdown, as seagulls swooped from out of the fog, in a 21-7 loss to the Yanks. Frankie would lead the Niners out of the tunnel, and charge onto the field from some spartan locker rooms shared by high school kids. And yet, for 25 seasons Kezar stayed the same. The stadium is ingrained in the city fabric, just as much as the cable car or Golden Gate Bridge. In some ways Kezar was awful. Uncomfortable, yes, but it was intimate. I remember parking was ridiculous. But, when I think back, one of the best things about Kezar, was as a neighborhood stadium. You could watch a game from the roof-tops of tall buildings embracing it. Kezar was a wonder for the senses."

-Jonathan Eggert

"The *Chronicle* declared on January 10, 1928, 'Kezar Stadium will be one of the most up-to-date, and architecturally attractive stadiums in the United States'. Parks Commission President, Herbert Fleishhacker added: 'Special attention is being paid to its attractiveness and, when completed, Kezar will be an object of beauty, as well as of utility'.
Object of beauty? That may have been a bit of a stretch.
On November 29, 1928, Lowell High School played Polytechnic High School in the city championship game known as the Turkey Bowl. The game drew 50,000 spectators, and is still considered the largest crowd ever at a Northern California high school football game."

-Bill Van Nickerson

"I was 7-years old when my father took me to my first Niners game in '64. It was a drizzly and overcast day. We parked our car in a resident driveway, just across the street from the stadium for $5. We got in line to buy two reserved seat tickets. In line was a guy selling trash bags used as rain gear for 25-cents, but we passed. Lots of fans were pushing from behind. There were no turnstiles, just one ticket-taker and his wooden box. We made our way to the North end zone of the stadium.

It rained off and on throughout the game, and the field was muddy. I remember there was only one bathroom, and it was a long way away. My father took me somewhere around the stadium on the field level. Once inside, suddenly, there was this big roar at the opposite end of the stadium. Then a bigger roar, but we were stuck in line in the men's bathroom. By the time we got back to our seats, a fan told us a Viking player scored a safety for us, and ran the wrong way! My father was so disappointed he missed the play. That must have been really something. It turned out to be one of the most outlandish plays ever at Kezar."

-Bob Kellerman

"

Kezar Stadium Facts

Location
777 Stanyan Street
between Willard and Frederick Streets

Area
Stadium - 7.55 acres -- 17.5 total acres, including
parking spaces for 300, and including Kezar Pavilion.

Length 820 feet   **Width** 550 feet

Seating Capacity
59,942 spectators, plus 320 press box seats
and 30 disabled seats in Veteran's Shelter

In 1957, my friends Lou, Gus and I ended-up at the Kezar Club across the street from Kezar, as the 49ers-Lions playoff was game sold out. All of us were blue collar guys, working as painters for the City. I remember by halftime we were blasted. The Niners were ahead 24-7, and everyone in the bar was going nuts. Then, in the second half they killed us. There were lots of swearing and bottles breaking. It really sucked. Everything went from an anticipation of a win, ready to explode, to something resembling a funeral parlor. No horn blowing, delirious screams of joy, jumping up and down in ecstasy - just silence. Even the confetti gun the waitress handed us to fire in victory, never fired. We saw dozens of police officers outside in helmets and holding batons - some on horses, some on motorcycles, waiting for a celebration or riot. It was heartbreaking. That is what I remember about Kezar."

-Joe McKinney

"A day after the 49ers NFC Championship game against the Cowboys in 1971, I was in an immense line of people outside the De Young Museum waiting with my mother for tickets to a

Van Gogh show. Saying to mother I'd be back in a bit, I slipped away and ran over to Kezar. Still quite young, I was able to slip through a fenced gate, walk along the inside corridor and through an entrance to the stadium. I wandered about the stands looking for any souvenirs from the game, maybe a discarded program. What I found was only a paper visor and lots of beer cups. I then went down the steps to the field. At the base of the stands in the East end zone, there was a tall chicken wire fence separating the stands from the track. I wondered why? I was told later by my dad that the fence protected players from garbage thrown by unruly fans. I never made it to a game on my own, but it was a great seeing the stadium. I made it back in plenty of time for the Van Gogh show."

-Rose Roemar

"I grew up in the city, and lived just few blocks from Kezar Stadium. As a teenager, I attended Poly High, which was just across the street from Kezar. Each day, I could look out my homeroom class window and see this giant concrete stadium. During P. E. classes, we had to run around the dirt track there, three times each day. Those who could not run, simply walked. What memories they are."

-Armin Sirjohn

"My brothers were born in Chicago, and I was the first family member born right here in San Francisco. My grandfather was a Shriner in 1954, and one year took my father, my three brothers and me to Kezar for the East-West game. I remember that specific day. Bart Starr was one of the quarterbacks. I was pretty young - maybe 12, and didn't know much at all about football. But, I was thrilled to be there. The West won the game, but I can honestly say, that day I was indoctrinated to football at Kezar. From then on, I was hooked on football, and ended-up with 49ers season tickets to Kezar in the late '60s."

- Jerry Wilkinson

"I do remember the bathrooms at Kezar were so overwhelmed, the urinals overflowed. One reason was guys would toss their cigarette butts in them. Some would urinate in the corner, and just ignore the urinals. It was that way almost every game. If you had to go, you made sure you went before halftime, or you'd miss half of the third quarter. In those days fans could bring in their own booze into the stadium, with the result that most were smashed by the fourth quarter."

-Mike Maier

"December 10, 1960, was the only day I attended a 49ers game at Kezar. The last time I saw weather conditions this bad was in college watching the 'Little Big Game' between St. Mary's and Santa Clara at Kezar in 1934. I sat through a rain storm, and watched a mud-battle.

Today was no different, as it rained cats and dogs. The 49ers were playing the Packers, and there was no grass in the middle of the field - just a sea of slop. As dreary as it was, 59,612 showed up, all huddling under umbrellas and protective gear. The game was a dud. The 49ers lost 13-0."

-Ken Goldin

3

The Experience

"In 1955, I joined the Christopher Milk Jr. 49ers Club, and with my parent's OK, hopped on a city bus, transferred to another, and arrived at Kezar Stadium. Did this a number of times that year, and only ten-years old at the time. The Jr. 49ers section was located in the West end zone, where we entered through Gate 21. A big event for us happened frequently. Whenever a field goal or point-after kick was made at our end of the field, a hoard of fifty or so fans would go after the ball where it landed, and a huge violent scrum for it would result. Lots of bruises, I'm sure. Once during a December game, an older guy muscled his way to the ball, ran off with it, then lateraled to someone in the stands. Next morning the *Chronicle* ran a picture.

The following season in 1956, Jr. 49ers were transplanted to a section located in the Southeast section of the stadium. It didn't take long to realize I could walk down a few stairs to below the stands, continue walking around to the other side of the stadium through no barriers, then upstairs and back into the crowd. I'd find a great place to sit in perfect view. The aroma under the stands - a mix of old concrete, cigarettes and stale beer - made the journey even more memorable.

Kezar officials got smart the following season in 1957, moving the Jr. 49ers section to the Northeast portion of the stadium (where the upper-corner juts above Kezar Pavilion). We were kept separate from the rest of the crowded stadium by a 6-8' chain-link fence extending from the field to the top of the stadium wall, penned-in like caged animals. Everyone remained in the section during halftime to hear ticket numbers announced for free autographed footballs. Several fans stood by the fence, itching for the moment to climb over, and get lost in the crowd. I actually tried it once. My one time kicked-out of Kezar.

One reason for wanting wider access to the stadium before the game ended, might have to do with cushions. Basically square, grey pillows, cushions were rented-out to fans for 30 cents apiece. At the end of the game, many of us gathered those left on seats, and redeemed each for 5 cents. We always made more than one trip, and many nickels. One game the cushion concessionaire for some reason decided not to redeem the cushions. A protest ensued. Cushion-renters flung them like frisbees, including several over the wall outside the stadium. Airing them out was a good thing probably. To no one's surprise, the ban was reversed the following week.

After games we also collected programs left on seats. I received a tip to not immediately head home after cushion collecting, yet instead go to the stadium parking lot, which happened to also be the location of both teams' locker room exits, cars and team buses. After getting showered and dressed, players would appear in the lot about the same time I'd show up. People of all ages – mostly kids – swarmed for

for autographs. Players back then were very willing to sign a program or football card - no strings attached. I felt fortunate to see and receive autographs from a considerable amount of players who eventually made the Hall of Fame. We related to the players via football cards – our primary visual connection. It was cool and exciting to suddenly see a familiar face, then be given his autograph. This experience added to the attractions each Sunday provided.

The 1957 season was special at Kezar. What occurred there during the final eleven seconds of a regular season game against the Lions goes down as my most thrilling game experience at Kezar. Tittle threw an alley-oop pass to R.C. Owens, which was caught for a touchdown. The crowd went wild, then silent for several minutes, more minutes, taking-in what had happened. I was in the Jr. 49ers section staring out toward the field with this feeling I'd never had before (felt it once more with Dwight Clark's catch). The '57 season's final game, a playoff with the Lions, was a sellout. General Admission had seats available starting at noon the Saturday before the game. A friend and I made it down to the stadium, and got in line along Frederick St. around 6:00 am. We had a good spot, yet had to wait six-hours, and endure pouring rain. I bought tickets for me and my dad, the only time he and I attended a 49ers game together.

By 1959, I was old enough to sell game programs. I needed a Social Security card, then show-up at this little building next to the stadium at about 8:30 am the day of game. I was handed a stack of 100 or so programs, and headed to a spot outside the stadium to setup shop. Older sellers, members of the concessionaire's union, were given preference for the best selling spots nearest Kezar. I found mine - the corner of Shrader & Oak along the Panhandle. Closer to game time, I'd move to Stanyan St., nearer to Kezar. Programs cost a quarter, and physically handling money, providing small change with dollar bills being handed me left and right, was a major effort. It's a wonder I was never robbed.

Highlights from selling programs during the years 1959-60 include the opportunity to sell during the East-West Shrine games, and the Oakland Raiders first season played at Kezar.

By 1961, I was hired to sell food items inside the stadium, with the opportunity to make more money than program selling. Having to carry a heavy load of soda turned-out difficult, and a sticky one at that. We wore blue smocks and little paper hats while climbing the stands yelling our wares. Moving up the seniority ladder, ice cream was easier to carry, went fast and was more profitable. Did that for a couple years, then I was off to college with sadly fewer visits to Kezar.

On a side note, there are a couple memorable events I experienced at Kezar aside from the 49ers part of the story. In 1954, representing Alamo Grammar School, I marched around the stadium participating in the San Francisco Unified School District's annual traffic boy parade. We entered Kezar through the same tunnel the players used to get from the locker rooms to the stadium. It was dark, spooky and very dusty. One classmate with asthma could hardly breathe. Years later in 1962, I quarterbacked for George Washington High in Kezar - against Lincoln High and Mission High. Playing on the same field, the same weekend as John Brodie, was a thrill."

-Bob Zingmark

"The highlight of my young life was always attending the 49ers games at Kezar. I worked very hard with my paper route to collect money from my customers, and had no problem spending it for an end zone ticket. Tickets were 50-cents, unless my neighbor gave me his extra season ticket on the 35-yard line. Often, I sat in the Christopher Milk section with a chance to win an autographed football. Never got one. Kezar was my second home during the '50s. I always went alone, which turned out to be a blessing. My grandfather took me to my first game at Kezar in 1953, against the Colts. We slaughtered them 45-14.

I could not afford a hot dog, so I brought my own sandwich from home. By the time the '60s arrived, I had more money to afford a hot dog and soda. I still feel today hot dogs at Kezar were best ever, accompanied with a steamed bun. I could also afford better seats, usually on the sunny (north) side of Kezar. Both the bathroom and the concession stand were underneath, where it was dark and kind of eerie.

After games, I would hop over the green railing encircling the field, and walk off with my heroes toward the tunnel. I got many autographs, and had mini-conversations with players. Once the stadium emptied, I would scan for discarded programs, ticket stubs, and cushions. I was happy as a lark riding the 33 bus to Mission Street, while reading the 49ers program, and looking at my autographs.

In 1964, I purchased two season tickets on the 15-yard line next to the Christopher Milk section (my current girl friend seemed interested where I was going on Sunday afternoons), and listened to Lon Simmons play-by-play on my transistor radio. From our seats, we saw people on rooftops watching games, just as they did at Wrigley Field in Chicago. Those fans had the best of both worlds. They could watch the game for free, and did not have to deal with the long ticket, bathroom and concession lines. Plus, they did not have to look for parking.

My trips to and from Kezar were an experience by themselves. I had to take the No. 52 bus to Mission Street, then transfer to the No.14 or No. 12 Mission to 16th Street, then board the No. 33 bus to Kezar. The bus was always late, and jammed with fans. Going to, and coming home from the games took two hours. Living in my neighborhood (Excelsior District), were Joe Perry and Forrest 'Scooter' Hall, famous for his drop kicks. He was also my basketball coach at Epiphany Grammar School.

The 1957 season was bittersweet. At the end of the season, we had identical 8-4 records as the Detroit Lions. The Saturday morning before the division playoff game, I got to Kezar at 6:00 a.m. to buy tickets for my dad and me, and it poured rain. I got soaked to the bone. With the

49ers leading Detroit 24-7 at the half, and the crowd going wild, tickets for the championship game against the Cleveland Browns went on sale. My dad gave me money to buy two of them at the ticket shack. Sadly, the 49ers lost the game, and my dad tore up his phantom ticket. Luckily, I still have mine after all these years.

The last time I visited Kezar in 1979, the 49ers held a scrimmage before the wrecking balls hit. I brought my two sons. It was very nostalgic. I always wanted to walk through the players tunnel leading to the locker rooms. My wish came true, when an employee of the San Francisco Park and Recreation Department allowed us to walk through it. I'll never forget that walk."

-Ed Cooper

"In 1953, when I was 10-years old, my family moved to the inner Sunset District of San Francisco. Exploring my new neighborhood on my prized flexi, I discovered only three blocks from my house a giant concrete monstrosity called Kezar Stadium. And, that it seated 60,000 people! This I found out, was the home of the San Francisco 49ers, a professional football team. And it wasn't long before I had a Sunday seat in that stadium, and was rooting for my new love.

Sitting in the Christopher Milk section, I'd scream my little 10-year-old heart out. But it wasn't all smooth sailing. The entire stadium was bleacher seating (no backs on any seat). The seats were numbered, but each number was about 18 inches apart, and if you had two people on each side with 25-inch butts, you had a problem.

Sometimes I would crawl over a railing, and sit in a space just above, where people entered the stadium. That worked well, until the one Sunday, I accidentally dropped my full large cup of Coca Cola, and it splattered on the head of an arriving fan, just as he was entering the section. An usher down below looked up at me, and unceremoniously tossed me out of the stadium.

Through foggy Sunday after foggy Sunday, my seat was in the end zone. But I never felt deprived. Scores of fans were sitting on the roofs of the nearby homes watching the Niners from much farther away than I.

I loved the games. The 49ers won some, lost some. I watched Gale Sayers one Sunday run wild over the 49ers, and remember one touchdown scamper where he started to sweep right, then spotting a flock of salivating 49er defenders, reverse his field, and weave his way to a 60-yard touchdown. That was talent to behold. I always looked forward to the game's end – win or lose. That's when I got a chance to make a little cash and fill my tummy.

After the game hot dogs, which hadn't sold for 25-cents during the game, were now available for a nickel each. One Sunday, I brought 20 hot dogs home, and my mom tossed 15 of them in the garbage. Those were different times in so many ways. The players worked for $5,000 to $10,000 a year.

Maybe the best thing different about those times, is the players were so much more accessible to the public then they are now. I have practically all my football cards from 1954 through 1958 autographed. On game day the players were permitted to park their autos just outside the stadium locker rooms. Other autograph hunters and I would gather by the players' cars after the game, and as the 49er players arrived, they politely took time to sign our cards and programs, while their wives waited patiently

Living where I did, gave me access to the visiting teams, who would come out in a big team bus on Saturdays, the day before the game. They'd practice at a small grassy area called the Triangle outside the stadium. At close range, I could sit there on the grass in awe, and watch the great Harold Hill gather in a long pass from George Blanda. And when the Chicago Bears practice was over, I could grab their signatures. As the season progressed, I got signatures from other eventual Hall of Famers: Frank Gifford, Lou Groza, Otto Graham, and Ollie Matson.

There was one more unanticipated advantage of living so close to Kezar – a great economic one for me at least. Fans had to scramble to find a place to park near the stadium, and were essentially at the mercy of us nearby home owners, who would charge extortionist prices to park their cars in our garages, or on our sidewalks. I was the oldest of four children, so dad allowed me to run the Sunday family parking business. Working it to the max, I could park four cars around our garage area, every time the 49ers played at $5 a car, a huge amount in 1955."

-David Kleinberg

"My older brother and I sold programs before 49ers games, and collected cushions at the end of the games. Ernie Freese was in charge of distributing programs to us. We'd earn 5-cents, for every two we sold, but we needed to be at least 100-yards away from a union man who'd be selling. I settled on the corner of Stanyan and Hayes Street, and my brother sold his programs next to St. Mary's Hospital, catching fans walking from Fulton Street. Once the game started, we got free admission into the Christopher Milk section, our pockets jingling with nickels. I had never seen so many people sitting in one place. The roar of the crowd at cavernous Kezar, the colors and sounds, the smells of stale beer and cigarette smoke, the players in their bright red uniforms captivated me. I was awestruck by the excitement of it all.

At one game, my brother was one of ten raffle winners chosen each home game to receive a Wilson football signed by all of the players - a treasured prize. He immediately tucked it under his jacket, fled to the exits and ran most of the way home. One afternoon, while fancying myself a pretty good punter, I kicked the ball up high into the middle of a giant palm tree just down the street from our home. Regrettably, the coveted ball is to this day enshrined forever, as an integral part of the tree, and my brother is still upset with me.

After most games, my brother and I snagged cushions for a nickel apiece. Working quickly was a necessity, because some older kids would try to steal pillows from us. After collecting our earnings, we headed straight to the player locker rooms adjacent to the Kezar parking lot, from where the players emerged ready to greet the fans. Crowds of kids would gather around the players in hopes of getting an autograph. Hugh 'The King' McElhenny was my hero. When he came out, he was mobbed by eager fans. I was so smitten not to leave his side, after he signed my program. Other boys came in for his signatures, but I was not about to let go. I just wanted to hold on to him. The King nudged me out of the way with a swift kick, freeing himself of this pesky gnat.

What exhilarating days they were at Kezar, the happiest times in my life with lasting memories forever."

-Henry Michalski

"It's game day, December 8, 1957. My friends and I are ready for the day's great adventure. Walking east on Lincoln Way towards Kezar, our pace is quick with the excitement of today's Baltimore Colts - 49ers game. The 49ers are in a tight race with the Colts and the Lions. We must win today to stay in the race. At this hour of the morning, the wonders of Kezar are all about. We are met by the first program seller, his foot resting on a large bundle of programs. The smell of boiled hot dogs is on my mind. Kids our age are holding signs out in the street. 'Parking $4.50.'

In the East parking lot we get in line for tickets. I eye the sign about the wire window. The last line in small type excites me: 'Under 12, 50-cents'. Gates open at 11:30 am. Game time is 1:30 pm. Once inside we run to a seat along the green pipe rail above the players tunnel. After an hours wait, a man opens up the gate leading to the field. I lean over the railing trying to see into the tunnel. Bodies press into me, pinning me to the rail. In the tunnel, there is a sound of shouting. The gold pants of the 49ers appear, glistening in the tunnel's dim light. Then they run past us in bright red and white jerseys.

Bob St. Clair signs his autograph for young fans after a game

The score goes back and forth. In the final moments, a rookie quarterback from Stanford wearing No. 12 throws a touchdown to Hugh McElhenny. It doesn't matter we didn't see it, because the action was at the other end zone. We're ahead. Moving down to the front row, I sit on the green railing eyeing the cyclone fence, which separates the field from the stands. The Kezar crowd counts down the dying seconds of a big win, as hundreds of boys assault the field in a mad dash. The fence shakes violently, and already kids are on the field. Across the field we run. Towering men in red and gold, sidestep their tiny admirers in a rush for the tunnel. My friends are lost in the crowd. The 49ers band plays in the background. The police begin to clear the field, chasing us off. I find my friends, and head for the parking lot to get autographs.

A large crowd lines the railing looking down on the walkway area, where the dressing rooms are located. I move with the crowd, following a player to a waiting car. I shove my paper and pencil toward him, as he finishes signing another piece of paper. 'Who's that guy?' I ask, looking at the scribble on my paper. 'There's Hugh McElhenny!' The tall dark, curly haired star of the 49ers carries a shaving kit and is immediately engulfed. I join the mob desperate to get his autograph. McElhenny keeps moving across the Kezar parking lot on his way to his Cadillac. Frantically, I push my paper and pencil toward him, but he keeps taking someone else's. As I near the white auto, I make one last desperate push. McElhenny stops to open the car door, then puts his arm around my shoulders and says, 'Next week son?'. He touched me, the great man touched me, and spoke to me! That was my moment of affirmation.

Moving ahead to October of 1967, I was quarterback for the Lincoln High varsity team, called the 'Brawny Mustang Flinger', as described by the *San Francisco Examiner*. We arrived at Kezar using Eastshore Lines No. 407, an old Muni bus, which contained our white-shirted varsity team. Down the stairs I led us past an old black man with a cigar who held open the door into the mysterious players' tunnel - the same used by the 49ers. Sunlight disappeared. It was dark, and the smell of dust was thick in the air. Bare light bulbs suspended from the ceiling. The tunnel bent to the right. My cleats sank into pebbled ground. I could see light. Closer to the tunnel's opening, I saw the green field, as bright sunlight bathed down on Kezar.

At 4:56 pm, on January 7, 1971, the Kezar clock wound down to '0:00' for the last 49ers game - Dallas 17, 49ers 10. A mixture of sadness and excitement fill the heart of this 49er faithful. Afterwards there would be no more 49ers pregame picnics in Golden Gate Park; no more difficult parking situations. Somewhere the last beer can rolls from the top rows of Kezar, under my bench, and comes to a rest at the bottom. I took one last look at the stadium and it's paint-peeling bleachers and empty stands, hard to believe this place was so alive with 49ers memories."

-William Fox

"The best job I ever had was from 1964 until 1970. I worked in the Kezar press box for a friend of my dad. We'd meet early then go into the press box and make coffee, and get hot dogs and sandwiches ready for the guests. The pay was a decent $20 per game. There was a kitchen under the front row of the press box with a stove, sink, refrigerator and counter space with electrical outlets for coffee urns. A couple of minutes before halftime, we would take orders for the food from the guests, then serve them. Once the game restarted, we would clean everything in the press box and the kitchen. Once finished, we were free to watch the rest of the game. A couple of times I went upstairs on the roof where the TV cameras were located, and got to see some instant replays before they were available to the TV audience. It was the best view in the stadium."

-Michael Lombardo

"While I'm happy the field at Kezar was named for Bob St. Clair, I'm glad the name of the old stadium itself didn't change. My heart was, and always will be with Kezar, which for 17-years was my fall weekend home. It was a magical, never-to-be forgotten shrine, despite it's often miserable weather, far away parking, rock-hard benches, and lack of precious amenities.

I was just a kid when Kezar became the hub of my world, and saw all the Niners games for more years than I can accurately count. I used my student body card to get into the games for 50-cents. I used to have a massive collection of programs from all of the games I attended. I gave them up a few years ago, but I'll never part with the memories. I think of one memory, and that spurs another one, and another, and I'm soon racing off on a journey back in time."

-Alvin T. Gutherz

"As a young female in the 50s, my dad had season tickets to the Niners at Kezar. Since my mom did not like football, it was my job to go with him. I remember every week having to sit on bleacher seats, squeezed between these huge men, friends of my dad, all smoking cigarettes or cigars around me. I couldn't stand the smell of the cigars, so most of the time I would go to the hot dog stands and buy food, just to get away from them. I really didn't watch much of the game, but I have to say, I did learn a lot about football in those days, and the only player I truly remember was John Brodie."

-Karen M. Warner'

"I grew up in San Leandro, and during the '50s, my dad and I took a bus from Villa Peluso's restaurant in Oakland to Kezar. Definitely the best of times with my father, and my favorite era of football!"

-Don Johnson

"If ever there was one for Niner fans before games, the Horseshoe Tavern on Chestnut Street was a 'regulars' bar for us. The owner was a former player of the 49ers. After we'd leave the 'Shoe', we'd make a pit stop at Leopard Cafe on Front Street, another Niner hangout. From there, we chartered bus take us to Kezar for home games. By the time we reached the stadium, we were all pretty gassed.

The exact years I visited Kezar are a little sketchy, but the players and events come into remarkably sharp focus. I lived for those games, every minute, every second. I never missed a single 49ers game going back to their first NFL season, and sat in the same seat, year in and year out. Section R row 28, right in the middle of the end zone. It was the best seat in the house. I even carved my initials into the bench. These days, everything about old Kezar seems like a highlight to me.

I saw the Rams Glenn Davis get his teeth knocked out from a Hardy Brown shoulder tackle. I was there the day Harry Babcock (the Niners bonus No. 1 draft pick in 1953) caught a last-second winning catch in a driving rain storm at the East-West game. It seemed every time we played the Redskins at Kezar, people picketed outside, because owner George Preston Marshall wouldn't sign black players. I saw Leo Nomellini play quarterback in an exhibition game against the South San Francisco Windbreakers.

I just loved going to Kezar, and can still hear the roar of the crowd, not to mention the music of the marching bands. Kezar was the best, by every test. Shoulder to shoulder, we stood among the best."

-Wayne Trimble

"I had just gotten back from the war, and it was a thrill to go to Kezar on Sundays. I only had to pay $1 to get in, and sit anywhere. I used to love watching Frankie Albert perform. The passing combination of Albert to Beals was as powerful as anything the Cleveland Browns had. The Browns were the dominant team in those days. In 1947, '48 and '49, I worked at the *San Francisco Examiner* promotion and sales department, and we always sponsored the opening preseason game with the Los Angeles Dons. At the game, I'd find myself in the end zone catching the drop-kicks and punts of Joe 'The Toe' Vetrano. I've had a very interesting career, going all the way back to the beginning in 1946."

-Lloyd McGovern

"As a Stanford alumnus, my favorite 49er was Stanford grad Norm Standlee. He was a popular fullback with the 49ers, and eventually replaced by Joe Perry. I was fortunate to be at Kezar in December 1950, for 'Norm Standlee Day'. About 20,000 fans showed up. At halftime, he was showered with gifts. I recall a few of them: five cases of Acme beer, a refrigerator, dinnerware set, golf shoes, and an Oldsmobile Deluxe Rocket 88 automobile. We ended the day beating the Packers 30-14."

-James Cox

"When I was nine years old, I went to my first 49ers game. I invited my dad, and 10 of my friends. We sat in the Christopher Milk section, and all had a great time. When I turned 16, I could no longer get into the milk section, so I'd wait outside the stadium for people to give free tickets, or would buy an end zone seat for 50-cents. If they sold-out, we found other ways to sneak into the stadium.

I knew a vendor who gave us his jacket and badge to wear, and I got in. It worked for a couple of games, until the gate men caught on. Some of my friends hid in the cushion cart, while the concessionaire would push the cart into the stadium. The funniest way we got in was the easiest. One of my friends bought a ticket and made it to the southeast side of the stadium at the 30-yard line. He would throw his jacket over the wall down to one of us waiting. Then we tied all of the sleeves together to form a rope, and one by one, each made our way over the 10-foot wall. Thirteen of us got into the game

My friend Gary didn't take many challenges lightly. Once he pulled off the best post-game dare ever. After a game in '58, we went down on the field, as there was little security in those days. I don't know what Gary was thinking, but the Bears beat us 27-14, and Gary was livid. He decided that, if he ran really fast, he could snatch the game football from Bears quarterback, Bill Wade, who was walking off the field holding it. Gary at 6-foot, 135 pounds, threw a body block right in front of Wade, who suddenly stumbled and fell down. Gary jumped up and ran. Wade was really peeved and yelled some obscenities, and threw the ball at my friend. Well, it must have made Wade more mad, because Gary caught the football, and ran away.

After games, we usually hung-out in the parking lot, getting autographs from players. One time the Packers bus was waiting right next to the visitor's locker room. We didn't see any guards, so my friend and I sneaked onto the bus, figuring we could get first crack at getting autographs from players boarding the bus. We looked out the window, and a policeman saw us. He was mad, and started yelling at us to get off the bus. Just then, a voice said, 'Don't be too hard on them officer, they're just kids. I'm sure they mean no harm'. We were shocked. It was coach Vince Lombardi. He asked us what we were doing on the bus. We told him we were waiting to get autographs. We asked him if we could have his, and he grinned, and said 'Sure, I'd be glad to, only if you boys promise not to pull a stunt like this again'. Outside the bus, some of the Packer players were watching and smiling. They knew how scared we were. I'll never forget that day."

-Jim Dickson

"To get to Kezar from my home, I'd either walk the distance, or take the No. 5 McAllister bus to Stanyan Street, then walk down the hill to the stadium. Kezar was not far from the Boy's Club on Page Street, where I spent a great deal of time during summers.

Usually the visiting teams practiced outside Kezar on Saturday afternoons, a day before the game. On one occasion the Redskins practiced inside the stadium. There was no security, so we walked through the tunnel from outside Kezar, right onto the field to watch. No one objected to our hanging out, as long as we were respectful, and maintained our distance. Some players would actually play catch with us, and allow us to shag kicks in the end zone.

The player who stood out most in my mind from that day, was Eddie LeBaron. He was great with us kids. He would toss the ball back and forth with us, and even make friendly conversation. Surely, such access to players stopped long ago, but we had our day.

KEZAR STADIUM

When I became 14, I sold programs. The city had a very tight union at the time, but they allowed a limited number of non-union kids to sell them. At first, it was a contest among age-eligible kids to get a few non-union program sales slots. I was pretty lucky, and I sold them regularly. I was loud and persistent in hawking my programs: 'Get your 49ers programs here. Only 25--cents!' Once the game started, we were allowed entry inside the stadium during the first quarter to sell. At the end of the quarter, we had to turn everything in. We were then allowed back into Kezar, unless the game was a sellout.

The 1957 season was both heartfelt and disappointing. I always enjoyed watching the 49ers play the Rams. First, the Rams had colorful players like 'Crazylegs' Hirsch, Paul 'Tank' Younger and Norm Van Brocklin. Secondly, they brought circus clowns with them, who livened-up the game. And thirdly, the Rams cool helmet designs with the horns were the best ever.

As a youth, I had an affinity for Howard 'Hopalong' Cassidy, the Detroit Lions running back. Everyone knew getting a ticket to the '57 49ers-Lions playoff game would not be easy. My plan was to become a scalper, and make a few bucks. The day of the game, I joined a long line outside the East end zone to buy four tickets. As soon as I purchased them, and moved away, the crowd rushed in pressing me into the wooden ticket booth, and literally lifting it off it's foundation. Then police on horseback moved in. I sweated the possibility I wouldn't be able to scalp my tickets. But, I sold all four quickly, and watched the game from the Christopher Milk section. I was a happier, 'wealthier' camper.

What a way to grow up. I have no maudlin regrets. The '50s were the 'Golden Age of Football', and a great time for kids."

-Michael Stern

"My father had season tickets in the early '60s, and could take his two boys to see pro football. We would park the car around Funston and Lincoln Way, which was a very long walk to Kezar for a young boy with short legs. We sat high on the north side, around the 10-20 yard line. Across the aisle from us was a group who very much enjoyed their pregame celebration, and carried it into the stadium, literally. The 49ers had a safety named Elbert Kimbrough. These guys called themselves the Elbert Kimbrough Fan Club. They each carried a 'first aid kit' with a red cross painted in the middle on a white circle, and the name of the club in a circle around that. Inside was a bottle, glasses, and related tools. As you can imagine, they were quite boisterous and emotional. Fights were not infrequent, and one day it spilled over the aisle, and I nearly got crushed by one of these buffoons falling after taking a hit. They weren't the only attendees in the stadium who fueled-up. At the end of the season, my father dropped his season tickets, as he felt the games had become an unhealthy place for his boys."

-Joel Wiener

"I am a native son of Palo Alto. My father was a big fan of John Brodie from his days down the street. Old Stanford Stadium was really something for us. Dad liked to take me to games at Kezar, in particular when the Saints were in town. We would pay someone $5 to park in his driveway on Stanyan or Page, and I'd wait while dad bought end zone tickets at the window. If I recall, the East end zone bleachers were pretty flat. And the game seemed far away. Football fans tended to be stocky, ruddy complexioned guys in pork-pie hats who took off their jackets, hiked up their braces, rolled up their sleeves, chomped on a cigar butt and kept their pint flasks close. I might have had a 49ers pennant, but swag just wasn't my thing. Later, when I had an income. I returned the favor taking dad to Candlestick games. By this time he was a big Bill Walsh fan. Funny for a Michigander whose blood ran Maize and Blue.

He's gone now, but those were good sports memories with him. It seemed to always be a sunny day sitting with my dad, while the guys around us yelled 'Ya Bum!'."

-Bill Comstock

"During the early to mid '60s. I recall walking onto the field after a game, and vividly seeing Leo Nomellini and Colts lineman Gino Marchetti walking together. Another time I won two tickets to a 49ers-Packers game. My buddy and I wore down-filled jackets, and entered Kezar with a couple cans of beer up each sleeve. My favorite memory occurred in 1969, as a high school senior. We picked-up a park bench in Golden Gate Park, when at that time benches weren't bolted or cemented down. We carried it to one of the Kezar gates across from the park, and were waved through, as if we had 'official football business' to conduct. We carried the bench down to the field, and spent most of the game roaming the sidelines. There weren't badges to wear, and security was much different than today. It was a dream come true being on the sidelines of a 49ers game."

-Paul Benson

"I grew up on 7th & Cabrillo in the '50s, and could hear the roar of the crowd at Kezar. My parents trusted me when I was eight to let me walk to Kezar with my friends and my Christopher Milk Junior 49ers Club ticket. After the games we would collect the seat cushions, and return them for the deposit with all the other kids. One year I met Charlie Krueger at the corner market on 5th & Fulton. I got a handshake, and an autographed picture. In the '70s, I worked for SF Park & Rec, and ran a chapter of the Junior 49er Minor Club at Glen Park and Sunset Playground. It was then sponsored by Berkeley Farms. I'm now 68, and still have my dad's season tickets, now at Levi Stadium."

-Fred Lawson

"The first game I attended at Kezar was an East-West high school all-star game, which took place sometime in late August in the mid-fifties. It was a cold and foggy evening, but exciting for a boy of ten, and just starting to take an interest in football.

My most memorable experience was a late fifties game against the lowly (then) Green Bay Packers. They had a new coach, and two new running backs. I was a member of a kid's band from Oakland, the 'Weldonians', and began performing during halftimes for the Niners. The band sat at the West end on the track, even with the end zone. It was an up-close vantage point. The sound of the players crashing against each other was deafening, as the two Packer backs shredded through the Niner defensive line. Not even the great 'Leo the Lion' could halt Vince Lombardi's smash mouth, nothing fancy offense.

While a member of the Weldonians we also performed at the first Raider game (1960), played at Kezar (Raiders vs. Lamar Hunt's Dallas Texans). There was hardly anyone in the stadium, but I was excited to see Don Sherwood and Y.A. Tittle at the game."

-John Stephens

"Win or lose, the 49ers always knew they had my support at Kezar. My love between the 49ers and Kezar began in 1955, when they were in the throes of a most dismal season. Every week, I wrote cards and letters of encouragement. I had my own battle with cerebral palsy, which became an inspiration to the team. I tried to never miss a game, and became an observer while sitting in the handicapped section of Kezar. I rooted hard for the 49ers, but will confess I had a special spot in my heart for Bob. St. Clair and Hugh McElhenny."

-Lisa Mellencamp

"I was an original member of the 49ers Majorettes Corps in 1953. We performed at every 49ers home game. Robert Olstead was our entertainment director, and he also organized our Corps. Many of us were high school girls, or had just graduated. We practiced Saturdays, and performed on Sundays. The girls were chosen out of several hundred students from the Olstead school.

Some say the Dallas Cowboys claim to have had the first NFL cheerleading squad. I have photos from December 1955, and September 1958, showing we did it first. In addition to twirling batons, we used flags, pom poms, umbrellas, ropes and sometime drums, as we marched up and down the field. At Kezar, we did both the pre-game and halftime performances."

-Deanna O'Mara Cope

"We lived on Fulton Street, across from the Buffalo paddock. In 1946, just before my 4th birthday, my dad walked me across the street to the Polo Field to watch the 'new team in town' practice. I cast my eyes on the red uniforms and was hooked for life. I got to meet Frankie Albert, Norm Standlee and Lawrence T. 'Buck' Shaw, a brilliant coach who featured some of the most explosive offenses in football history. I was given a helmet by Standlee. We attended practices often, but my dream was to go to a game at Kezar Stadium.

The greatest victory I witnessed at Kezar, occurred on my 7th birthday. Frankie Albert outplayed the Cleveland Browns Otto Graham, and the Niners ran up 56 points in a 56-28 win over the perennial champions. The West end was a dangerous place to be late in games, if the 49ers weren't winning. As the beer flowed, tempers would flare and often bottles filled the air. There were a few memorable fights, such as the riot that occurred against the Philadelphia Eagles. Hugh McElhenny defended himself by swinging his helmet at two Eagles defenders who had jumped him. Fans emptied on to the field in a free-for-all that lasted close to 15 minutes.

Many humorous memories linger from Kezar. One season, running back J.D. Smith got his first carry from scrimmage, after signing two years earlier as a defensive back and special teams player. J.D. had bugged the coaching staff for two years to let him run the ball. That day, among his carries was an 86-yard jaunt around right end for a touchdown that earned him a starting job, and he led the team in rushing the next five straight years. On this particular play, he circled right end on the heels of guard Lou Palatella. I was lucky to have a bench pass for the games that season, as a result of playing golf with the 49ers ticket manager at Harding Park. As J.D. circled the end he quickly sped past Palatella, and broke into the clear. With J.D.'s speed, Palatella was panting down the sideline behind him yelling, 'Slow down you SOB', and Leo Nomellini was roaring with laughter on the bench and making fun of his fellow Italian.

Another memory of Kezar was seeing fans sitting on the rooftops of the buildings across the street. It was a time to remember."

-Gary Mialocq

"When I was on the Safety Patrol squad at Ross School in Marin County in the early '60s, one perk given me was membership in the Christopher Milk Junior 49ers Club. One weekend a dozen of us piled into Vice-Principal Fitch's '57 DeSoto station wagon, and headed to Kezar. While scouting for a parking space in the park, we noticed people parking all over the place – flower beds, etc. Once in the stadium, we headed to our seats high above the East end zone at the rim. I remember watching a seagull about 30-feet away making slow progress against the wind. When the visitors took the field (I can't remember who), there were a lot of sparkles above the West end tunnel - beer and whiskey bottles hitting the chicken wire strung overhead for protection. After the game the Faithful were well lubricated, many giving sustenance to the trees in the park. A great day at Kezar.

For decades I thought I might have been making this up, until a couple of years ago my friend, Noah Griffin, told me everything I recalled was correct. Noah was in high school then, and remembered the little kids in the Jr. 49ers Club way up in the sky, and the chicken wire and sparkles over the tunnel – 'a lot more graphic up close', Noah said!"

   -Ben Ballard

"I was eleven when I went to a 49ers game against the Detroit Lions in October, 1966. The Lions had a brand new kicker, Garo Yepremian. My memory is it was his first NFL game. He was a huge novelty because he kicked soccer style. I think he was the first in the NFL (Gogolak and Stenerud were AFL). No kids played soccer at that time, so he was a huge novelty for us. Why do soccer kickers kick sideways? Additionally, he was a foreigner! I believe the Lions won that day, and my feeling was they had been bad sports."

   -Tim Mitchell

"I went to my first games, as a boy-scout usher in 1956 and 57. I saw all of the 49er greats of the era through the late sixties, sitting in the end zone for 50-cents (12 & Under), and went regularly through high school (SI) and college (USF). Saw the advent of the 'Alley-Oop' in 1957. I remember Owns making an alley-oop catch over Bob Boyd of the Colts - probably 1960, and Boyd kneeling on the ground, pounding the turf in frustration. We used to be able to run out onto the field after the game, and jog next to the players heading for the locker room. I hung out in the parking lot, and got autographs from the players from both sides. 'Big Daddy' Lipscomb was one of the nicest, most accommodating guys I remember. Played on that field for St Ignatius, as part of the 1962 and 1963 undefeated teams. It was a huge thrill the first time I ran out of the tunnel onto the field. I played in one of the great prep games later, the 1968 WCAL Championship with Dan Fouts (SI) and Lynn Swann (Serra). Missed the last two years of Kezar, as I was in the Army. I listened to the final regular season game in 1970, in Vietnam on Armed Forces Radio, as the 49ers beat the Raiders to get into the playoffs - all those years at Kezar, and I missed this big win! Still a Niners fan with season tix at Levi -- in the end zone of course!"

-John Tastor

"In 1959, the 49ers were playing the Colts at Kezar. Red Hickey was the coach. The 49ers had an all-alphabet backfield - all the guys' names were letters: Y.A., C.R., J.D., and R.C.

Yelberton Abraham (Y.A.) Tittle played quarterback; Raleigh Climon (R.C.) Owens was flanker; Cornelius (C.R.) Roberts played fullback, and running back J.D. Smith used his initials only. The backfield only lasted a short time, as Hickey installed the shotgun formation using three quarterbacks."

-Jim Fosbury

"Kezar was quite an adventure for John and me. We thought Kezar was the best in the West, although the bench seats were pretty uncomfortable, and close together. All players' wives sat in the same section. Everyone dressed nicely, and some of the older wives wore fur coats. They were so nice, and included me right away in the group. A few of them used to stop at the Kezar Club across the street from the stadium for a cocktail or two before the game. I was only 20 at the time, and I thought they were so sophisticated. Ruth Carol Nomellini and Shirley Wilson were such fun. We always brought umbrellas with us, because of the seagulls it seemed were forever present. We were in the stands when Tony Morabito had a heart attack in his box, and died. It was a huge emotional blow. He was well-liked by everyone in the organization.

Y.A. Tittle and John Brodie

We would often get tickets for friends and family. One time, I had about 14 tickets to pass out in the Kezar parking lot to family and friends, and hadn't kept one for myself. I went to the box office, and they gave me another. During the '60s, it was such an adventure to drive through the Haight Ashbury, and look at all the hippies, singing, dancing in the streets. My kids would hang out the car windows and gawk at them.

The 'boo birds' at Kezar became part of our experience with lots of anger directed toward John over the years. They were relentless in the end zone, where the beer was flowing throughout the game. It was hard when our kids got older, and had to witness this. I think I hit someone some unruly fan with an umbrella once. There was a man a few rows in front of us who always booed John. His name was Ernie. Someone told him that John's kids were sitting a couple of rows behind him. To his credit he quit booing. One time John was heading back to the locker room with John Unitas, and told him to put on his helmet. When asked why, John said fans throw beer bottles, cans or other objects at the players. Just then a can came down on Unitas' head. After that they put up a screen over the tunnel entrance. It seemed there was never a dull moment at Kezar. We shared a lot of memories there during the 14 years John played."

-Sue Brodie

"I lived near St. Marys College, and for two summers as a kid, I was Len Rohde's 'personal' carry-guy. One preseason, 1965 or '66, my dad took me to a exhibition game versus the Cowboys. It was close, and the Niners had one chance to win at the end of the 4th Quarter. Brodie launched a perfect pass to Kay McFarland in the corner of the end zone. Touchdown! Kezar went nuts. Wait...flag on the field - holding on #76 (Len Rohde). No TD! Kezar then went really nuts. I had never heard swearing like that. Dad grabbed and pulled me aside, as a 12-pack of Hamm's Beer from a few rows up slammed into where I had been sitting. The game was then called due to fans 'disagreeing' with the call, and hurling bottles onto the field. The next day at St. Mary's, I grabbed Len's helmet and pads, and we quietly walked to the practice field. I innocently asked him, 'Did you hold him?' Len looked me in the eye and said 'No way. It was a clean block.' Quite a Summer for me!"
-John Boresen

"I'm an 81-year old 49er fan. Right after the war my father was an MD at Letterman General Hospital in the Presidio. We lived at Park Merced - at the time housing for military officers. Frankie Albert, the star QB of our new football team, the San Francisco 49ers, who was my idol, and lived close by. I went to all of the Kezar games with Frankie and his wife Marty. What a thrill for a 7-year old. I remember the NY Yankees and Buddy Young, the LA Dons and all other teams of that league.

Marty told me if we lost, to NOT talk with Frankie on the drive home. But, if we won, I could talk all I wanted. I still have his original Jersey #63, before the new numbering system started. I'll always remember the wonderful times at Kezar, and sitting in the players' family bleacher area. Lots of fond memories with players who would show up (next door) for adult beverages, and talk about upcoming games. My dad used to take 16mm movies of me playing with the players on the big lawn in the complex. Frank would throw me the ball and the players would pretend to try and get me as I ran for a touchdown. Johnny Schields, John Strzykalski, Alyn Beals were all there, and at times even Buck Shaw.

It was a sad day when the Alberts moved to Palo Alto. We followed a year later when my dad went into private practice there. We remained close, and Frankie would take me to baseball games and football practice sessions at Stanford University, his alma mater. I do remember the vendors there, and what Marty would let me order. What a great era."

-Rush Faville

"I recall growing up in Canada, and watching 49er games from Kezar on Sundays late in the season. Lots of seagulls and muddy uniforms, but a very interesting stadium."

-Jim Waters

"Living in Mill Valley in 1970, there was a Jr 49ers Minor Club. At the club you would meet a player, watch an NFL film and get a ticket to a game. My brother and I walked five miles at night to the meeting. At the time my mom was dating my stepfather, who was a staunch 49ers supporter with season tickets to the 49ers at Kezar. Since my mom and dad were going, we would go with them. I remember the first time I saw Kezar, I was afraid Dick Butkus was going to be there, although the 49ers were playing the Cleveland Browns in the first game of the 1970 season. My stepfather bought me a 49ers and Redskins pennant.

I remember for my birthday getting the *First 50 Years* book. I would look at the pictures and be lost in the game. The description of Hugh McElhenny: 'ran with a rare grace and elusiveness', was the best ever. I also watched the NFL highlights with Pat Summerall and Tom Brookshire. The next day my friends and I would play football in the rain, and run all day pretending to be Gale Sayers or John Brodie. I was hooked.

My memories are so vivid of the Minor Club, and my first trip to Kezar. I relate the story many times. NFL football is responsible for me having a childhood of fun and excitement."

-Kevin Scanlon

"When the Detroit Lions played the 49ers at Kezar on December 22, 1957 for the right to be in the championship game against the Browns, we blew a 17-point halftime lead and lost 31-27. The Lions quarterback Tobin Rote was bigger than General Motors. Their Coach, George Wilson, became more important than the new Fords and Chryslers. A ticket to the 49ers championship game, which were sold to the public at halftime, were about as valuable as a street car transfer. I'll never forget how disappointed I was after that loss. I saw on TV that the come-from-behind Lions win at Kezar was ranked No. 2 in the NFL's top-ten greatest comebacks. Sad, but true."

-M. Bishop

"My most memorable Sundays at Kezar were the annual Alumni Day celebrations, held at the end of the year during halftime. The Niners would invite a large group of former players, and they were introduced one by one. Before the game, the alumni and their wives would have a special pregame breakfast meal at Rickey's in San Rafael. The Bay Area guys would show up in force. Notable players were Norm Standlee, Alyn Beals, Nick Feher, Lowell Wagner, Bruno Banducci, Eddie Forrest, Jesse Freitas, Visco Grgich, Rex Berry, Paul Salata, Ken Casanega, George Maderos and Gail Bruce to name a few. I remember Frankie Albert didn't show up one time, because he was in St. Louis doing his weekly TV show."

-Homer L. Biggs

"In 1958, I attended my first 49ers game at Kezar. The Packers were in town, and my dad was a season ticket holder. We sat in the 66th row, the very top of the stadium, on a crowded backless bench. Steps leading to the top were steep and never-ending. My dad loved those seats, I remember him saying, 'You can see the entire field from here. You can lean back against the concrete wall, and there's no one behind you, if you want to stand'. All I knew it was usually cold and windy up there, and players looked like ants. When I complained about not being able to see well, dad would give me his binoculars. He told me to keep them focused on the tunnel, because soon the players would be coming out.

Moments later an announcer began introducing the 49ers players, as there names were called out one by one. The roar of the crowd was thunderous, almost frightening. There names were all new to me: Tittle, McElhenny, Perry, Nomellini and St. Clair. My dad referred to them as 'YAT, The King, The Jet, The Lion', and 'The Geek'. They all ran to the sunny side of the field, but one player in particular stood out among all the others, literally heads and shoulders above the rest. Dad said his name was Bob St. Clair, and at 6-foot-9 was the tallest player, and best blocker on the team.

To say that I was in awe of this player would have been an understatement. With my dad's permission, I ran down the never ending flights of steps to the bottom, where the steel railings separated the fans from the field. I flung my legs underneath the lower bar and sat down resting my arms on the railings. As I scanned the 49ers bench, I found myself focused on St. Clair. But, this time it was something other than his size that caught my eye. It was his jersey number 79. My birthday was July 9 (7/9). I thought that was pretty cool. At the end of the game, I asked dad if I could meet St. Clair, and get his autograph. As a typical 50s dad, he responded in a sympathetic voice: 'The players don't want to be bothered after the game. They're anxious to get home, to their families.' Dad worked for the *San Francisco News-Call Bulletin*, one of the city's major newspapers. The following day after a game, he brought a surprise home for me. He had obtained a publicity photo of St. Clair for me from the sports department. I ran to my bedroom and taped it to my wall. As fate would have it, 41-years later (ironically, at the age of 49), I was working on my doctorate degree at the University of San Francisco, and my first authored book was born. It would be the story of the 1951 USF football team called *Undefeated, Untied and Uninvited.*

What's also ironic, is St. Clair was a member of that '51 team, and I scheduled my first interview with him. Although my anxiety level was at an all-time high, the interview went well. Bob had resurrected my youth - of a young girl sitting by the railing at Kezar watching my hero, and all the exciting memories he had given me.

Bob St. Clair was not just a great football player with a great personality. He became a true and valued friend for years."

-Kristine Settle Clark

"My dear friend Granville (Gran) DeMerritt, was a longtime usher at 49er games at Kezar, and the head usher for many years. He and I were great friends, and for years he came over to my house in San Rafael on the day of a home game. Under the influence two or three cups of coffee, I drove him to and from Kezar.

Gran often told stories about his service as an usher, and one of them is quite memorable involving the passing of 49ers team owner Tony Morabito in 1957, during a home game against the Chicago Bears. Tony was stricken with a heart attack in the press box, and Gran working there, ran down the Kezar steps to the 49ers sidelines and to doctor Bill O' Grady, whom he escorted to the press box. O'Grady treated Tony before he was transported to a nearby hospital, where he passed away. After O'Grady brought back news Tony had died, the 49ers became very emotional, overcoming a 17-7 halftime deficit to beat the Bears, 21-17.

Memories come back to me in waves. I conversed with John Woudenberg at a 49ers alumni dinner years ago, and asked why he retired from pro football after the 1949 AAFC season. He answered he could make as much money, if not more, with a business career, and wouldn't subject his body to the type of abuse he suffered on the football field.

Later, I became a 49er press box aide, conducting post-game interviews in either the home locker room, or that of the visitors. Back in the day, the various 49er PR moguls allowed me to interview players of my choice, usually the quarterback, and players who made key plays.

I was often asked by visiting radio or TV to do stats or serve as the spotter. The late Jack Snow, a color commentator for the Rams broadcasts, teased me for eating a hot dog with ketchup instead of mustard during halftime. Paul Salata and Billy Wilson were two of the 49er luminaries I was pretty chummy with in the press box. I've lived in San Rafael for nearly 50 years, and being a 49er game day helper, I also drove longtime 49er stadium announcer Dave Scofield, who lived in Corte Madera, to and from the games.

While seeing the 49ers beat the defending world champion Lions, 24-21 in 1958, I asked myself, 'why couldn't they have done this in the 1957 playoff game?' I couldn't help but think at the time, if the 49ers hadn't blown their 20-point lead in the second-half, they would have easily defeated the Cleveland Browns in the title game like the Lions did. In the 1960s, when I was a Kezar vendor, I remember cornerback Jimmy Johnson being my favorite 49er ... despite the explosive play of John Brodie, Dave Parks, Ken Willard, Bernie Casey and the rest of the high-powered offense. I remember Alvin Randolph returning an interception 94 yards against the Bears, and from my vantage point as a vendor, Randolph was running in my direction. It was a huge thrill."

-Ron Lent

"Watching games as a youth at Kezar remains memorable to me for three reasons: glare, the Leopard Cafe and Wayne Tarr. Longtime 49ers fans will still recognize Tarr as the team's unofficial cheerleader, and I mean that in the most flattering way possible. Tarr, with his distinctive beard and voice, did something cheerleaders of today rarely do: He actually led cheers.

The Leopard Cafe was the downtown restaurant, where my dad would attend 49ers booster-club meetings. My dad, mom and I went to the Leopard for breakfast with other fans, then took a bus to Kezar. In some sense, it was more special for me to go to the Leopard that day than to go to Kezar. I had been to probably a half-dozen 49ers games, but had not set foot in the famed Leopard Cafe.

I don't recall too many particulars from the games, except the 49ers couldn't stop anybody. They were considered entertaining, but hardly considered contenders. We sat in the Northeast part of Kezar, called the Christopher Milk section for regular-season games. I remember trying to watch games with an almost unbearable glare coming from the setting sun. At age 11, my eyesight must have been a little better than that of some of the adults sitting near me. I do recall some grown-ups thanking me for telling them what happened on a few plays."

-Steve Kroner

"Going to the games at Kezar with dad was unforgettable. I was 19-years old during the 1952 season. The fans were really excited about our team. Hugh McElhenny won Rookie of the Year, and became one of my favorite 49ers of all time. He really ran well, as did Joe Perry, 'The Jet'. I especially remember the last game of the season against Green Bay. Three original 49ers from the AAFC days called it quits. One was John Strzykalski, who had been a star halfback before McElhenny came along. The others were quarterback Frankie Albert and team Captain, Norm Standlee. Standlee had contracted polio, and broke his hand in a preseason game. The highlight of the game was at halftime. As Joe McTeague's 49ers band played 'Frankie and Johnny', Albert and Strzykalski came out of the Kezar tunnel. Standlee didn't show, but fans roared like crazy. A spirited 49ers beat the Packers 24-14. It was a memorable day."

-J.R. Tomlinson

"I've been a rabid 49ers fan for over 60 years, and originally from Baltimore. When the Niners and Baltimore played each other at Kezar, the rest of Sunday afternoon was all about hot dogs and beer. In fact, as a kid I was an absolutely an enormous Colts fan. I always had terrific admiration for their players - Johnny Unitas, Lenny Moore, Raymond Berry, Gino Marchetti. After our move to Daly City, my allegiance turned to red and gold. My mom's side of the family are all Niners fans, but my stepdad still likes the Colts. My mom sits upstairs watching the Niners on TV; he sits in the basement. Footballs creates anger in our family, but Niners football rules!"

-Harold Kramer

"Scofield Arms was the name given to the Kezar press box to honor stadium announcer, Dave Scofield. Joe McTeague was the original 49ers band leader, and before the game his band played the National Anthem, and at halftime 'Sweet Georgia Brown', and 'When the Saints Come Marching in' (before the New Orleans Saints became a franchise), while they marched on the field."

-Frank Del Norte

"I attended Poly High, across the street from Kezar Stadium. As soon as I acquired a camera I started photographing while in my teens. After a stint in the Army Air Corps, I approached the San Francisco 49ers organization in 1948, and became their 'de facto' team photographer. I immediately began taking photos for them at Kezar. There, I started my long career with the 49ers, shooting on-field action at every home game, while moving up and down the team's sideline. Kezar was the perfect place to shoot photos, because I could reposition myself throughout the game with easy access from the running track. I documented all the 49ers home games at Kezar until 1971, when the team moved to Candlestick park. During those formative years, I developed an intimate bond with the 49ers and their fans."

-Frank "Rip" Rippon

"My first season as a Kezar vendor was in August, 1966. I was 15. All the newbie vendors gathered at the Gate 11 and were called out by seniority. I honestly don't remember if my name was called, or someone just pointed me out. I was first assigned soda. I was around 5-foot-3 and maybe 120 pounds, and each load of soda had 40 - 10 ounce cups. Now that wouldn't have been too bad, but the tray that held two rows of sodas was made of metal making it really heavy. Walking the steep steps at Kezar was a chore, although every 10 steps was a platform landing to rest. If you ever walked them, you know what I'm talking about.

So here I was, hawking sodas on an overcast day. Certainly I wasn't going to make any serious money. I worked on 20% commission, same as the hot dog and beer guys. Sodas sold for 25-cents, a nickel a 'pop'. Climbing the steps, I wasn't shy, as I yelled 'Soda, soda here!'

I was amped, yet worried, because I was yelling to a sparse crowd along with the seagulls. It took almost 30-minutes before some fan bought an orange soda. My first sale ever. He was very kind, and told me to sit down and take a break. We talked for awhile and I left.

I made it through the day, and sold four loads. I cleared $5.00 and change. As time went by, I sold hot dogs, and made decent money. Over the years, I had some great moments vending and met so many great fans"

-Gordon Analla

Hot Dog Facts · 1957 Season

· A Kezar hot dog "hawker" sold an average of 10 to 20 loads per game (60 hot dogs per load)

· A fully-loaded vendor's bin weighed 30-pounds

· On average the "hawker" walked 4-5 miles per game, up and down the steps

· During the 49ers-Lions NFC playoff game, fans consumed a record 11,781 hot dogs

---

"My uncle Bob took me to my first game at Kezar in 1956, at the age of 12. The game was against the Browns. Immediately, I became a Hugh McElhenny fan. Watching him run with the ball was special. It was like he did everything himself. On one particular play, six Browns surrounded him, and 60-yards later he scored a touchdown. The way he used his blockers was amazing. My uncle said he was the 'King' of the halfbacks, because of his classic running style.

In 1961, when he returned to Kezar as a Minnesota Viking, he dazzled the crowd. On one play he made his way past his former team-mates, fending them off with his signature straight arm for a 32-yard touchdown. My memories of 'The King' will live with me forever."

-Roger Bias

"It must have been around 1963. I was a Camp Fire Girl, and we formed an all-girl drill team, which was part of the halftime show at Kezar. In less than a generation, 49ers halftime entertainment went from family entertainment to Las Vegas type shows."

-Sally Reinhardt

"I became a Niners season ticket holder in 1947, and will admit I only missed a handful of games the following 50-years. When I married my wife in '51, she told me, 'I do not like football, because I don't understand it, so don't buy me a ticket'. The following year, I bought season tickets again, but this time she went to the games with me, and have ever since. After games, we'd meet the players and have our pictures taken with them. My wife got to meet coach Buck Shaw. We were very fortunate to see all the Niners victories at Kezar."

-Betty and George Carlson

"My dad, Anthony Messina, met Joe DiMaggio at a Kezar game in 1949. He sat with my dad and his group. The 49ers were playing the Yankees, and Joe signed my dad's program which I still have today. Dad said Joe was old-fashioned, looking like he just got off the banana boat."

-Debbie Lorio

"At 10 or 11, my brothers and I would hitchhike to the games from Burlingame after church. Then, we would try to find a way to sneak into the games. One gate man knew our family, and allowed us in, if no supervisor was around. Sometimes fans had extra tickets and gave them to us. I remember one game, 49ers Norm Standlee was knocked out cold. We were told he had swallowed his tongue. A trainer had to knock out some of his teeth with a knife handle to pull out his tongue. Standlee finished the game, and we learned he had swallowed a chaw of tobacco."

-Jim Monahan

"One memory of Kezar stands out. I was at the Niners first regular season game in 1950 against the Yanks. We lost 21-17 to those New Yorkers. The lowlight for us, was the punishing running of the Yanks, Ace Parker and Spec Sanders. Their one-two punch kept our Bay team off balance the whole game."

-Hal Hornburg

"It was a magical time when my dad would take me to a 49ers game. I was 8 at the time. Going across the bridge, dad would let me pay the bridge tool at the toll gate. We would usually park at Fulton and Arguello in our cousin's garage, and walk to Kezar. Before the game was the best part, as dad let me ride the merry-go-round in the Children's Playground across the street from the stadium. The deal was I could ride the carousel, and buy some pink popcorn only before the game, but not afterwards. We had to be ahead of the traffic to get back across the bridge."

-Dorothy Brenner

"I went to an exhibition game at Kezar in 1954. It was against the Fort Ord Army Training Center team. I have always remembered that game, because their best player was Ollie Matson, who was drafted by the Cardinals. I sat on benches at the East end. I don't remember the score, but that day made me a Niner fan forever. Years later, my grandfather got me a seat in the press box. What a thrill for an 11-year old."

-Glen Hilton

"I started going to Kezar when I was seven-years old in 1954. After the end of that first year watching the games, my dad asked if I was serious about the Niners, and I answered yes. The next year, I had my own reserved seat in section LL row 8, seat 1. The ticket cost $3.50. I remember that, because I still have the stub."

-Mario Aliota

from left: Hugh McElhenny, Joe Perry, Y.A. Tittle and John Henry Johnson

"I went to the games from 1954 to '56 to watch the 'Million Dollar Backfield' of Y.A. Tittle, Hugh McElhenny, Joe Perry, and John Henry Johnson. What a bunch of great players they were. Today that backfield would be called 'The 100 Million Dollar Backfield'."

-Joyce Miller

"My father and I had a rigorous, yet gleeful schedule on Sundays in the Fall. We would attend Mass, go back home to watch Lindsey Nelson's taped highlights from the previous game, then climb into our station wagon, and caravan over to St. Mary's Hospital, where my father worked as a pathologist. We'd park our car there for free on game days, and walk to Kezar. In '67, those few blocks from the hospital to Kezar were among the most bizarre blocks in the city - lots of hippies and street vendors trying to sell their wares to us. We did manage to buy game programs on the way. It was an experience for sure. The games were great. Win or lose we had a wonderful time."

-Terry Jeffrey

"In the mid '60s, my two Lincoln High school buddies and I had season tickets in section UU for three years. Over the long seasons at Kezar, we really got to know fellow season ticket holders. After the third season, a friendly couple behind us said they were not going to renew their season tickets. We were shocked and immediately wanted to know why? Their answer was hard to digest. They were giving up their 49ers tickets to buy season tickets for this brand new franchise in the East Bay called the Oakland Raiders, and we never saw them again."

-Robert Cooper

"I lived with my aunt and uncle at the corner of Haight and Shrader, an easy walk to Kezar. On game days, they let me park cars, room enough for three cars in their garage, at $3 each. In 1955, nine bucks for a 10-year old kid was a fortune. My uncle had season tickets for my brother and I on the 48-yard line, right under the press box. During games, I always got splashed with beer from the drunks in the stands, and remember the bathroom was always flooded. I'd have to look for another one, which seemed like a mile away. My brother, who was 12-years older than I, said many fans would head to the Kezar Club after the game, and heartily drink more beer."

-Bob Burke

"The last season the 49ers played at Kezar in 1970, I broke my leg in October, but desperately wanted to continue going to the games. I don't recall if it was the city, or SFPD, or the 49ers, who allowed me to drive right up to the gate on game days, so I could hobble on my crutches up to the handicapped area on the North side of Kezar. That year the 49ers made it all the way to the NFC championship game. I only missed one game, because of my surgery"

-Tim Pennell

"My story begins in 1951, five years after the 49ers made their nest at Kezar. Up to that point, while living in the city, I followed local high school football rather than the Niners. However, that all changed the day my wife presented me with a birthday gift - Niners season tickets. She rues the day she did, as I renewed my tickets every year for the next 33 years. Kezar was really a crap-hole, although it was easy getting 20,000 fans into a half-empty stadium. The benches were hard, the food was cold, and there were long lines at the men's room. The only way I survived the cold and foggy weather was to drink lots of coffee. There was a lot of spirit at the games, and I loved watching the Niners."

-Henry Paddia

"I was raised in So. Cal., and grew up a Rams fan. I never got to see the Rams play live, until we moved to Palo Alto, and my parents bought 49ers season tickets. In 1957, I was at the game when 49ers R.C. Owens made an alley-oop catch to beat the Rams 23-20. It was even a bigger thrill, when dad bought tickets to see the Rams play the 49ers in a basketball game. Dad told me in those days most players needed extra money just to make ends meet, and every dollar mattered."

-Rob Stone

"What made watching the Niners at Kezar, were the refs letting them play the game. They might throw a flag here and there, but they let the players go toe-to-toe, swinging, clubbing each other. I remember once McElhenny getting wrestled to the ground, only to get away until his forward motion was stopped. And, it took a host of tacklers to do that. I also saw lots of contact with receivers and defenders running down the field. It was really fun to watch back in those days."

-T. Grigsby

"I still have the memory of standing outside the official's locker room in the belly of Kezar, adjacent to a parking lot to watch Gil Stratton conduct the CBS Sports halftime show. They were using a corkboard to display the day's scores."

-Michael Fritz

"My first time going to Kezar was September 17, 1961, quite an experience. Before the game against the Redskins, about 50 protesters from the Congress of Racial Equality (CORE) were picketing outside Kezar at the East end of the stadium. They were protesting against the Redskins being the only team in the NFL to not hire black players. They were waving banners and signs shouting 'Redskins Unfair', 'Racial Equality,' 'Join the Protest' and others. We did make it through the crowd to the gate entrance, but it wasn't easy. There were about 40,000 in attendance, yet more attention was paid to some of the protesters who got in, than the game itself. By the way, the 49ers won 35-3."

-William McNair

KEZAR STADIUM

"I was in the 5th grade, and remember going to Kezar with my friend, whose father was a ticket manager for the 49ers. We sat in the 'Jack Christensen' end zone seats. After the game we got to go in the locker room. It was a lot of fun."

-Robert Krepelka

"We lived at Alma and Stanyan across from Grattan Park, five blocks up the street from Kezar. In our backyard was an old horse barn. Between the barn and the small back yard and driveway, I could park 10-12 cars. Drivers would self-park, as I didn't drive. We charged a buck a car. That gave me enough money to buy a seat at the game, and some food - especially if there were smaller import cars to park that day.

When the 49ers played at Kezar, it was a great era, not for the team's success, but for just how rough and tumble an NFL game and the city was. Kezar had no luxury suites, just a press box. Everyone sat on a wooden bleacher bench with no chair back. My clearest memory of the games was against the hated Rams.

I had to leave the stadium before the game ended, and mayhem began. A few minutes before the two-minute warning, all the police would disappear into the Kezar tunnel, and re-emerge wearing yellow rain slickers and helmets. Then I'd see beer bottles start flying, generally aimed at the police and visiting team. There would be fights in the stands between fans. It was like that almost every game. It was definitely not the wine and cheese set.

Once I got home, I had to hop a fence to get in the back door. Inevitably the first car parked it seemed, was always the first guy's to show. The car was buried in the back yard, and he couldn't leave, until the other cars backed out. I hid until they all left. My parents didn't help at all. They wanted nothing to do with it. Boy, those were crazy days."

-Sean Hallinan

"In 1964, I remember going to the Jack Tarr Hotel to purchase 49ers season tickets from their headquarters. How times have changed. Counting preseason, there were 10 games, but I paid for only the six regular-season games. I paid $30 for a seat on the fourth-row behind the visitor's bench. My good friend Ralph bought a season ticket, as well. We bought the same seats the following season, but I went into the service for two years. After discharge, I resumed going to games. What stands out in my mind most from those years was the guy sitting behind us. His friends called him Smitty. He and a friend would carry an ice chest filled with food and booze to each game. Smitty was real generous with the beer. As often as he did, he'd fall forward and neither of us could stop his fall. Ultimately, Smitty once landed on this lady, and it was bad timing on his part. She told an usher, who escorted Smitty out of the game."

-Case Nelson

"I think it was 1959, when a train load of us Rams boosters came up from LA on Saturday, for a 49ers game the following day. I remember it was my 21st birthday. Some of us left for the SF International Airport to greet our beloved Ram players arriving on a chartered flight. The next morning, buses from Gray Line took us to Kezar. We sat with the band members and cheerleaders halfway up in the West end zone.

At first we all thought Kezar wasn't a bad place. It brought out a community feeling. What I remember were those beer cans rolling down under my seat from above us. Throughout the game, we had to duck from flying objects, like ice cubes. Though I was cautioned, some drunk 49er fan poured a whole cup of beer over my head, and my jacket got completely soaked. It was the worst embarrassment of my life. To add insult to injury, our team did not score one point, as the 49ers beat us 34-0. I never went to another game in San Francisco."

-Sandy Rasmussen

"I was at Kezar for the Niners first game vs the Chicago Rockets in 1946. We won 34-14. I saw the 49ers first complete pass, their first tackle and Beals make our first touchdown catch from Albert. Those wooden benches gave me splinters, but Kezar was intimate. You could almost touch the players, and see expressions on their faces. Being a Stanford grad, my heroes were Albert, Standlee, and Banducci, and later Brodie, who took a lot of abuse from fans. I never missed a single game at Kezar. The stadium was a place ingrained into the city's fabric.

Even locals packed the roofs of apartment houses just to watch the game. The best thing about Kezar, it was a neighborhood stadium. My biggest thrill was meeting the Niner players up close at their annual Chamber of Commerce luncheons at the Mark Hopkins Hotel. I went from table to table, and mingled with Stanford grads who were my heroes."

-Harry Guido

"I sure miss Clementine, the Niners donkey mascot. She wore an old gold miners blanket on her back, and was quite an attraction for the fans at Kezar. When the Niners scored a touchdown, she's kick up her back heels with joy!"

-Barry Harper

"My dad worked for Les Vogel Chevrolet back in the '50s, not far from the 49ers headquarters at the Jack Tarr Hotel. He would get us free tickets to see the games at Kezar. Going to the games, I always remembered the narrow streets jammed with cars. It was total chaos. Fans came by bus, trolley, bicycles or walked to see a game. Once inside the stadium I noticed those omnipresent seagulls flying around looking for food, as they retreated to nearby rooftops across the street from the stadium. I still have stirring memories from games against the Rams, Bears, Lions and Packers. Still, the action at the games weren't always restricted to the field. There was plenty of activity from the fans in the stands. After a loss, 49ers players were a constant target for fan abuse, ducking beer bottles and ice cubes, as they made their way off the field. There seemed to never be a dull moment at these games."

-Jim Hoslet

"I was born and raised in Syracuse, N.Y., escaping the cold winters there to come to San Francisco in 1966. The football we watched in Syracuse were the lowly N.Y. Giants and Buffalo Bills, when O.J. Simpson played for Buffalo. After a few years, I bought tickets to see the Niners play at Kezar, and remember parking was a hassle. Though, once inside the stadium, seating was relaxed and rather snug. I overheard two fans talking how the Niners needed a new coach. One guy was all in for hiring Syracuse 'Orangemen', Ben Schwartzwalder. I nearly fell off my seat. I knew who Ben was - a great coach, but known as old school, two yards and a cloud of dust. The forward pass, it seemed, was prohibitive from his playbook. Luckily, it never came to pass. The 49ers eventually hired Dick Nolan. Bless my stars."

-Don Cogswell

"In 1948, my dad took me to my first Niners game at Kezar. We ended up buying tickets from a gate man for a couple of bucks. All the ticket booths were closed that day, as the stadium broke an attendance record against the Yankees. Over 60,000 packed the stadium. A lot of the fans were sitting in the aisles, and in folding chairs on the track. Dad said our head coach was the first coach hired in the whole AAFC. We beat the Yankees 41-0. The Niners plain lowered the boom on those guys. Albert had four touchdown passes, and Jimmy Cason and Forrest Hall looked swift playing running back."

-Elmer Truttmann

"Before I attended my first game at Kezar, I played a lot of football in vacant lots and the sand dunes at Ocean Beach. In 1960, my brothers Tom and Jim were too young to attend 49ers games by themselves, so my dad bought tickets for us to the games. Before a game, dad would usually stop at the Lucky Club, or Murio's on Haight Street. Dad later said they were bookie joints, where he placed bets on games. I still have a ticket stub from my first game, section UU, 42nd row. We had lots of company and the seagulls joined us, as well."

-Ray Collins

"Kezar was a lovely place. The grass was bright green in August, and the fans cheered loudly, especially when Frankie Albert bootlegged the ball. The hot dogs always tasted better at a game. The 49ers had one player, Paul Salata, who was a movie star in the off-season, and their tackle Bob Bryant was a stunt man in Hollywood. When I got married in 1951, I converted my wife from being a fan of the symphony and opera to an avid Niners fan."

-Orvell Peterson

"I attended a game at Kezar with my dad one season. Three memories stand out on my only visit to Kezar. Before the game we saw a guy holding a sign that read: $5 to park in someone's driveway, on closer inspection this guy had a crowbar in one hand, and a sign in the other. So, we passed on that one. I also vividly remember how the fog would roll in late in the game, so heavy it was difficult to see the players on the field. And lastly those ominous seagulls dropping their turds on people's heads. Luckily I wore my cap."

-Steve Peterson

"I have a vivid memory of old Kezar Stadium. At games, when nature called, it seemed ever-present seagulls weren't particular where their droppings landed - even if they fell on players' helmets. 49ers Bob St. Clair said he didn't know it most of the time where the seagulls dropped their waste, until the trainers told him to look at his helmet. 'Will you look at that!', St. Clair said in disgust, while pointing to his helmet covered in seagull castings. If you going to honor something that stood the test of time, St. Clair Field sounds so much better than 'Seagull Excrement Field'."

-Dick Brill

"My friend Ray and I attended the 1971 NFC championship game at Kezar between the 49ers and Cowboys, and though it was a monumental disappointment losing to the Cowboys, what really impressed us still etched in our minds: recording artist Johnny Mathis sang the National Anthem. It was awesome. Mathis is a native San Franciscan, and attended George Washington High School."

-Larry Finch

"I attended my first 49ers game in 1949. What a thrill it was. I was like a kid waiting for an early Christmas. The night before the game, I couldn't sleep. The three-hour drive from Chico, where we lived, was worth it. I was full of anticipation. The price of tickets was reasonable: $1.20 for General Admission. The 49ers won the game 42-7 over the Chicago Hornets, which made it even sweeter for me. Two years later, my parents moved to the city, which made it much easier for me to get to Kezar. I became a 49ers season ticket holder for the next 21 years at Kezar, until the 49ers moved to Candlestick. I cherish those wonderful years going to the games."

-Louis Darnell

"I remember how excited I was to go to Kezar the first time in December, 1952. With dad holding my hand, my amazement and wide-eyed look at how big the stadium was to this 7-year old kid, is enduring. Score-wise, it was not a good day for us, but I really caught 49ers fever. Thanks to dad, it only got better. Bless him for giving me this gift of love which has lasted for years. Often, I look through the program dad bought me from that game, now part of my 49ers man cave."

-Casey Mendell

"During the 1957 season, my dad and his three co-workers had season tickets to Kezar. As time went by, two of the workers passed on, and surprisingly, my dad had kept all four season tickets. Our next door neighbor, my sister, brother and I used the tickets for a number of years. We sat in section SS, row 48, all of us in the same row. That season was one of the best ever. We made history with the alley-oop pass play from Tittle to Owens. We beat the Rams, Bears and Lions with the alley-oop, but lost a heart breaker to the Lions in the playoffs. My sister cried, and of course my dad, brother and I were quite depressed."

-Bill Hogan

"Memories of Kezar? There are so many, but the one which first comes to mind happened in 1964. I still see Vikings head coach, Norm Van Brocklin running down the sideline waving his arms, trying to get the attention of Jim Marshall, who was running the wrong way. He reached the end zone, and tossed the ball away in celebration, thinking he scored a touchdown. Although, Marshall's run, while memorable, didn't hurt the Vikings. They still beat us, 27-22."

-Bob Fouts

"Kezar is immortalized! I still remember the original backfield of Frankie Albert, John Strzykalski, Norm Standlee and Len Eshmont. Buck Shaw with the beautiful silver hair was the head coach. I saw the original T-formation Albert ran with a full-house backfield. At the time they were in the All-American Football Conference."

-Bill Patterson

"Today, many people complain the City has changed, giving the implication all old and familiar touch tones of their lives have been swept away. Many have, but the spirit of Kezar Stadium never will. If you were lucky enough to witness a 49ers game at old Kezar Stadium, you are one of the fortunate. Kezar was a home-grown neighborhood stadium, a jewel in the city. You'd maybe have to jump on a streetcar or bus to get there, but there was none of this corporate stuff going on back then, like there is today. At Kezar, you sat on wooden benches, and you urinated in a trough, and the fog and seagulls rolled in by the fourth quarter. Players like Frankie Albert, Joe Perry, Leo Nomellini performed. It was where the 'Million Dollar Backfield', and 'Alley-Oop' were created. I remember the 'Red Dog' - a linebacker blitz. I saw legendary Sammy Baugh, Ollie Matson and Buddy Young play at Kezar. After games, we'd go to the Kezar Club, a shot and a beer place. It was part of life, and the whole experience. What memorable days they were."

-John Burton

"I'm a 62-year old San Francisco native who grew up in the Sunset District. My unique memory almost seems like a dream now. My dad and I took the 72 bus to a 49ers games in the '60s. In those days the goal posts were made of wood, not built in metal cantilevered over the goal line like they are today. One game in particular at the end of the season, we beat Green Bay in a thriller. Fans literally knocked the goals posts down, as I guess they wanted a piece of history to take home with them. On the bus ride home, one fan was showing off his prized souvenir piece of wood from the goal post. It's no wonder the NFL did away with these disposable goal posts for metal ones."

-Curt Cournale

"My parents lived in Twin Peaks, so it was easy for them to get to the stadium. They told me stories watching the best of the best players at Kezar. They said before Montana and Rice, there was Frankie Albert, Y.A. Tittle and John Brodie, and receivers like Billy Wilson, Gordy Soltau, Dave Parks and R.C. Owens - players my parents loved reminiscing about. Kezar was a special place for fans and football."

-Kelly Fisher Hester

Radio Play-By-Play Announcers

1946-48	**Bud Foster**	KYA
1949	**Bud Foster**	KSAN/KSBR
1950	**Rod Hughes**	KSAN
1951-53	**Bud Foster**	KYA
1954	**Fred Hessler**	KFRC
1955-56	**Roy Story**	KFRC
1957-59	**Bob Fouts**	KSFO
1960-71	**Lon Simmons**	KSFO

"I remember walking to a game with my boyfriend sometime in the mid-60s. It was drizzly, and the 49ers really played badly. There must have been about 25,000 empty seats, except for the seagulls occupying a bunch of them. I think the 49ers had won just a couple of games that season. That day my boyfriend said they lost again. I must have fallen asleep, because I don't remember there was anything to cheer about."

-Betty Hoslet

"One Sunday, a couple of friends and myself came up the bright idea we could rent neighborhood driveways to some of these wanderers. We charged a $1.00 to park. The parking spaces we sold were neighborhood driveways. I don't remember if we ever got caught doing this. I think I only participated in this once, but others continued doing it for years."

-Anthony Miksak

"One year, we had a family discussion about whether we could afford the luxury of season tickets. In the late '60s, we'd drive from Redwood City, with no clear plan what to do on Sunday. And, if nothing presented itself, we were drawn to Kezar to watch the 49ers. We would walk-up to the ticket booth, and pay $6.25 for a reserved seat. And once inside Kezar, we'd pick a seat wherever we wanted."

-Corey Farley

"I was privileged to see Joe Perry play at Kezar in 1963, his last season with the club. I actually met him at of all places, the Brentwood Bowl in South San Francisco. He bowled in the same league as my dad, a fanatical Niners fan. I mentioned to my dad the guy bowling a couple of lanes away was Joe Perry. He called Joe over and introduced me. My dad, nonchalantly referring to No. 34, as just Joe. Wow!"

-George Smith

"On August 28, 1955, at age 16, I saw my first game at Kezar against the Browns. It was cold and overcast, and we sat in the East end zone. I read about Joe 'The Jet' Perry in the newspapers. To see him in person was a real thrill. Not only did he have a big day, gaining over 100 yards in 17-14 win. It was 'Joe Perry Day.' During halftime, Norm Standlee was the MC, and along with other admirers, bestowed a truckload of gifts on him. I specifically remember Perry getting a bowling ball, and lots of appliances. After the game, I waited to greet Perry, in hopes of getting his autograph. About 1,000 others had the same idea, but eventually, I made my way through, and Perry signed my program."

-Tommy Gin

"I remember when Monty Stickles joined the 49ers, and became one of Brodie's favorite targets. I sat in section PP at Kezar, when Stickles scored a last-second touchdown catch from Brodie to beat the Lions. After that I became a big fan of Monty. I remember he ran a Big Brother type program for kids without fathers in the off-season, and my good friend Charlie Whitmore was one of them. When Stickles appeared at Winston Market on Hickey Blvd. in So. San Francisco, he was so kind to the kids. I did notice he had a granite jaw, as he signed his football card I brought along."

-Joe Olbinski

"The last game of the '61 season was probably my biggest thrill ever. There were five of us kids competing in the western regionals finals of Ford's 'Pass, Punt and Kick Contest.' I was eight-years old, and told around 25,000 others across the US had tried out for the chance to compete. I didn't win, but my 26-yard punt tied for the best mark. The distance was measured by the nearest half-foot. My pass reached 24-yards, a personal best for me. After the contest we got our pictures taken with three judges, all former 49ers: Frankie Albert, Ed Ballati and Dutch Elston. The best part is we all were given a McGregor white football with facsimile signatures of NFL greats- Johnny Unitas, Y.A. Tittle, Bart Starr, Don Meredith, John Brodie and others."

-Jeffrey Lieberman

"In the 1940s, my dad was an air-raid warden in the Mission District. After the war he and his uncle brought their hand-cranked air raid siren to Niner games at Kezar. They hid under their over coats and clamped it down on the wooden bench. They would wind it up and let it rip during every Niner score."

-Norbert Feyling

4

Christopher Milk Section

"As a youngster, my mother often called me to walk to a nearby Richmond District grocery store and buy milk. I made a point to buy Christopher Milk, so I could cut the free 49ers coupon off the back of the carton. A couple of times in the late '50s, I incurred my parent's wrath, because milk spilled all over the kitchen floor after I used scissors on the carton, which was not empty.

Sitting in the Milk section at the games, I remember watching Y.A. Tittle and Hugh McElhenny. Long before the term 'alley-oop' became synonymous with dunking a basketball, Tittle and wide receiver R.C. Owens invented the play on Kezar's turf, using R.C.'s leaping ability. He was able to snag lobs from Y.A. in the end zone. I remember Steve Spurrier started six games in his first four seasons, as the 49ers quarterback. In addition, he served as the team's punter."

-Hal Morris

"I was about 13, and at each game it seemed the Christopher Milk section attracted a new group of juveniles, all thinking the same thing. Groups became so large, more police were referred there, obstructing us from retrieving a football on the field. Still, my friend made it through the assemblage of cops, scooped up the ball after a missed field-goal, and made it back into the stands with the prize. He never got caught. After the game, we spent hours of fun tossing the ball around."

-Roger Barkoff

"I grew up in walking distance of Kezar, and saw many 49ers games in the '60s and '70s. I was lucky to get Christopher Milk free tickets on occasions. When the visiting team would enter the field from the tunnel, there was an opening in the fence where I could see them close up. I would get to the games early enough, so I could get a good spot on the railing. The best day was when Vince Lombardi was coaching the Redskins, and they were walking right by us, and I yelled 'Hey Vince!' He looked up, and waved at my dad thinking he might know him. For a kid to get that close to real NFL players was a dream come true."

-Gene Immendorf

"I took the Muni across town from Bernal Heights with Christopher Milk tickets in hand. Then, while being so close to the field, watching the teams warm-up was a dream come true. It was really special. Although the Milk section was fenced-off, shortly after kickoff, we would sneak under the fence, and often end up sitting between the 30-yard lines. Ushers didn't try too hard to stop us, or return us to our section, since the crowds were not overwhelming. After games I remember walking off the field with players, particularly Hugh McElhenny with his arm around me. Perhaps I'm romanticizing the memory, since it was such a wonderful time in my youth."

-Al Waxman

FREE 49er FOOTBALL TICKETS

Once again, Christopher Dairy Farms is pleased to invite the young people of this area to be our guests at all 49er home football games (without cost) at Kezar Stadium.

Any youngster or group of boys and girls may be admitted at the games free.

We are happy to have you as our guests!

• OFFICIAL TICKET FOR ADMISSION •

Christopher Milk carton panel featuring free ticket

"I started going to Kezar with my brother in 1965. I was 10, and he was 12. My mother would drop us off, then pick us up after the game. We received free tickets, and sat in the Christopher Milk section. After the game, we would all gather in the parking lot for autographs from the players, because they had to walk to their buses or automobiles. My fondest memory was beating the Green Bay Packers 21-20 in 1966. The fans swarmed the field, and tore down the wooden goal post. What a scene that was. I went home with a small piece of the wood. I also attended Saint Ignatius High in the city, and all of our home games were played at Kezar.

-Brian Hull

"When I was nine, I would buy a quart of Christopher milk, which cost about 15-cents. Then, I'd pour out the milk and clip the coupon off the back to get into a game. The Christopher Milk section was supposed to be for kids 16 and under, or something like that. Once I got into the section, I realized age didn't matter. There were guys old enough to be my grandfather sitting there, drinking whiskey or beer and smoking cigarettes. It was a dangerous place."

-Bill Baxley

"We lived on Clayton Street in the '50s, and Kezar was the outer limits for a freewheeling childhood. I can remember the size and shape of the black stenciled numbers and letters on the concrete walls indicating entry ways to the seats. I was an avid member of the Christopher Milk Jr. 49ers Club, and eventually found myself with a free ticket, sitting near the end zone before a game. I remember watching Y. A. Title warming up. I was amazed he was bald, and taller than I had imagined. The whole thing was very exciting. Hugh McElhenny was my hero, and later at Lick Wilmerding High School, I emulated him playing halfback."

-Ruben Carter

"In the 50s, my friends and I went to Kezar, specifically in hopes of retrieving a football from a PAT or field goal attempt, before the referee had a chance to get to the ball. Sitting in the Christopher Milk section in section RR, in the Northwest end zone, before they moved us to the East end zone, made it was easy for us to hop the short railing and rush onto the field before the kick."

-Harvey Mandell

"We kids in the neighborhood signed up for the Christopher Milk Club program. The seats were in the end zone, where it was really rowdy. My best friend's dad used to take us to the games in his big station wagon. It was so much fun. I'll never forget one game when we went down to watch the players walk through the tunnel to the locker room after the game. John Brodie I think had a broken arm, and my best friend's dad asked him, 'How's the arm John?'. He answered, 'Getting better!'. That was the biggest thrill for us kids, plus seeing all the players with mud and blood on their uniforms was really cool! Of course, after the game the seagulls would nail us when we were leaving the stadium. It was so funny to us kids to see who would get pooped on."

-Charlie Greene

"I remember going to Sun Valley Dairy at 25th and Lawton, and getting free Christopher Milk tix to Niner games in a fenced section in the East end zone. You'd get in free, then hop the fence and go anywhere. Still, those seats in the Milk section were decent. After the game, we'd collect cushions people rented for the game. With a buddy, you could make a couple of bucks out of it. Also as a teenager, it was easy to go to one of the concession stands and buy a beer, as there weren't lines, and all you needed to do was hand the money to the worker, and take off with the bottle."

-Dennis Danziger

"We started going to Kezar in the early '60s, and sat in the Christopher Milk section. The 49ers always had a good offense, but lacked a good defense. We'd get a lead, but were never able to hold it. I remember a tie against Green Bay, and always losing to the Colts and New York Giants. During these years, the stadium was usually half-full - maybe 30,000 fans, and during a critical part of the game, the crowd would be silent, and then you could hear booing. This happened often."

-Harry Franco

Christopher Milk milk carton featuring collectible player pictures

"I was also a Christopher Milk kid with free tickets to years of great football, while taking the N Judah right to the game. After the games we collected seat cushions for a nickel apiece. The adults would bring boxes of booze. When a bottle was empty they would let it roll down the steps. You'd hear the glass smash down at the bottom. Years ago, the NFL did a story saying the first tailgaters were Vikings fans. I called that BS!

I wrote to NFL films, and told them the Vikings didn't play their first game until 1961. I told them back in the '50s, Niner fans would drive to Golden Gate Park the night before the game. Each fan had their own parking spot. After Mass, they'd get driven back to the Park and tailgate. 49er fans were the first tailgaters. About a month later, I received a letter from NFL Films which said I was right. Sadly my letter was lost in a house fire. But, I will always be proud I called BS to NFL Films. I was born September 2, 1946, the time my 49ers played their first game."

   -Kev Kelly

"I had a San Francisco newspaper route, and was assigned to sell papers outside the stadium on game day. One year, someone gave me four free tickets to the game. My uncle George formed the '35th Avenue Booster Club.' If he got 13 kids to go with him to the games, he got in free in the Christopher Milk section. I lived on 15th Avenue, but he recruited me. We sat in the corner near the end zone. We were fenced off, and could not move to other parts of the stadium. My high school, Sacred Heart, used to play all our home games at Kezar. In Fall of 1960, we played Saint Ignatius High. At the time our SH football team was not particularly good, and we lost to Sl for the second-year in a row by a large difference in score. SH students streamed out onto the field, and tore down the goal posts Saturday before a 49ers game. The papers said SH fans took out their wrath on the goal posts. They had to erect new goal posts in an emergency, for the 49ers game the next day. SH paid for the goal posts, and students were assessed a fine by the administration."

   -Ray Gilmore

"It seemed every kid loved Hopalong Cassidy. During halftime on Boys' Club Day, about 2,000 of us in the Christopher Milk section got up, and screamed in cadence, 'Hoppy, Hoppy, Hoppy!'"

   -George Smith

"For big games cars would park on Lincoln Way, all the way down past our house on 25th Avenue. Fans would walk or take the No. 72 bus to Kezar. We'd cash-in soda bottles for 3-cents and a nickel for the big bottles, and buy a Christopher Milk carton of milk. We would clip the coupon off the back and sit in the milk section at Kezar. After the first quarter, we'd either sneak over the cyclone fence, or talk somebody into sliding their ticket stub through the fence before halftime. Then we'd walk through the gate, and find a seat near the 50-yard line. It was so cold one game, and there was no hot chocolate left. I had my first and only cup of coffee. I haven't had a cup of coffee since, unless it had a little Jameson or Bailey's in it. I credit the author of this book, Martin Jacobs, who has kept my brother and me, and other neighborhood kids enlightened to the greatness of Kezar and our 49ers. He helped make us all 49ers fans forever!"

-Geoff Smyth

"My family could only go to a 49ers game if we had the Christopher Milk carton tickets back in the 1960s. I remember when we finished each carton of milk, one of us four kids would be so excited to be the one to cut out the coupon on the side and save it. We lived in Midtown Terrace below Sutro Tower, and very lucky it was but a 2-mile walk to get to Kezar, or a quick bus ride. No parking nightmares! We kids were free, independent. The seats were always on the very sunny Northeast side of the stadium, near the end zone facing into the sun. Sun or no sun in our faces - it was such an exciting rush to see the 49ers play!"

-Alice McCaffery

5

The Games

Hugh McElhenny

"I witnessed the 49ers first NFL Championship game at Kezar in 1971. By all accounts, the setting sun played a role in the 49ers effort against the Cowboys that January day, but my memories also include the distinct unsettling caused by a full can of beer whirling within inches of my left ear at the game's end.

I was a paying customer that day, seated on one of the crowded, backless benches in Kezar's East end zone, near the Flying-A scoreboard. Many newspaper accounts mention the near-riot in the West end zone at the end of the game. I can attest matters on the East side were definitely plenty hairy.

The one play I've remembered over and over again, occurred early in the third quarter. From about midfield, John Brodie threw to a wide-open Ken Willard. As the ball was in the air, one could see from the

East end zone Willard coming toward us would have clear sailing, if the pass was completed. Then Willard lost the ball in the sun, a drop. It was a 'what-if?' play. For years, I wondered what Willard thought about that play. Reached at his home near Richmond, Virginia, Willard said, 'I remember it very well. It was a play where John rolled right and I snuck out on the left side. The sun was lower. It was just sitting on the rim (of the stadium). I looked back, and just didn't see the ball at all, until it was too late. That play stuck with me. I don't know if I would have made it (to the end zone), but I would have been down there a long way'.

We were probably a better football team that day. Cowboys running back, Duane Thomas, was in his rookie year. Walt Garrison, Cowboys fullback, played with a bad foot ... he took a shot to play that day. Of all the times we played them, it was our best chance to beat them."

-Pat Sullivan

"In December of 1957, I was discharged from the Coast Guard, and a group of us attended the 49ers-Colts game at Kezar. The game was a sellout, and we bought end zone seats. In that game, Brodie threw a touchdown to McElhenny for the win, with less than a minute to play. McElhenny, to whom this hero business was old stuff, was still mighty nice to watch. He beat the Colts Milt Davis out of his socks. For Brodie - a rookie - he had to throw it then or never. We won 17-13, setting up a showdown with the Packers. It was also 'Billy Wilson Fan Appreciation Day.' He was one of the greatest receivers the 49ers had during that era. As I remember, Billy cleaned up with gifts that afternoon in pregame ceremonies, with a motorboat, new golf clubs and many more gifts. Coach Frankie Albert commented in all his years of football, high school, college and pro, Billy Wilson was one of the greatest competitors he'd ever seen. I'm still hoping some day he makes it to the Hall of Fame. He deserves to be there."

-Sal Valencia

"One memorable Sunday, in 1960, I remember fondly an overcast afternoon at Kezar. Not only did we beat the Bears handily 25-7, but on this day before the game, the Tony Morabito memorial bench was dedicated. Three years earlier, he suffered a heart attack while sitting in the press box during the Bears game. Sixteen 49ers from that 1957 game showed for the dedication. It was only fitting Billy Wilson, who caught the winning touchdown pass for the 49ers against the Bears that fateful day, would be part of the ceremony."

-John Mellekas

"I watched my 49ers first game at Kezar in 1950, against the Yankees. But, they came from the AAFC, so that hardly counted. The second game I watched against the NFL Chicago Bears was a different story. The Bears won the game 38-13, but that wasn't the real story. The competition was between quarterback Frankie Albert, who used the modern T-formation, and Johnny Lujack, your typical prototype quarterback, as seen today in the NFL. They were both great.

Two plays taught me how football was really played. They took place right in front of me at the East end zone of Kezar. Lujack was terrific, while looking everybody off to his right, he'd come back across his body to his left, and complete a pass for a first down. The other play I saw, Albert called a student body right. He took the ball on a bootleg, hiding the ball behind his hip, literally, and ran to his right untouched into the end zone. The play seemed to work all the time. Albert was so smooth. The seagulls would line up on the 10-yard line like a wire, and when the action came to our end, they would go to the opposite side of the field. Besides the game, there was always a wonderful halftime. This game the Chinese girls' drum team and the Glockenspiel Corps from Old St. Mary's played 'The Bells of St. Mary's'."

-Richard Falvey

"In 1960, when I was a youngster, my dad took me to my first 49ers game at Kezar against the Green Bay Packers. After the game I went down on the field. I looked up, way up, at Bob St. Clair. Although, he's 6-foot-9, he looked 15-feet tall! He was real sweaty and muddy. He scared the heck out of me, and reminded me of the Incredible Hulk! It still is etched in my mind. After St. Clair retired, I dropped by his liquor store in Noe Valley for a second look. To my surprise, sitting behind the counter in a chair, he looked like a regular dude."

-Henry Lefebvre

"My father took me to two 49er games at Kezar Stadium. My first was vs. Baltimore, November 16, 1969. I was 13-years old, and an avid pro-football fan. I posted the weekly NFL standings page from the *Sacramento Bee* on my bedroom wall, and hung little plastic helmets for all teams according to the standings. This was my first time in a stadium larger than a small-town high school football field. We parked some distance from the stadium, but still early. I was impressed with how big Kezar was inside a continuous oval. I was surprised at how much more colorful the grass and uniforms looked than on television.

The other game I saw was vs Los Angeles on November 29, 1970. Kezar still seemed quaint and antiquated. The weather was drizzly. Our seats were about the 5th row near the 20-yard line on the visitor's side. There were a lot of Rams fans around us, and scattered through the stadium. Two 49er fans paraded around the stadium in front of the first row with large banner reading something along the lines of '49ers - Super Bowl, Rams - Toilet Bowl' (with a drawing of a toilet). I was excited to finally see my heroes in person, particularly John Brodie, Gene Washington, Deacon Jones and Roman Gabriel.

What made the biggest impression was Deacon Jones knocking Brodie down repeatedly. Brodie took quite a beating from the much larger Jones. During the game the friction was increasing between 49er fans and Ram fans. When the game ended there was a huge brawl in the stands behind the far end zone, with beer bottles flying back and forth between sections. That was my last impression of Kezar."

-Greg Hull

"Yes, I was at Kezar for 49er games during the 1956 season. I went with my boyfriend. He was a staff sergeant in the Marine Corps, and carried the colors at the beginning of the game with three others. I was so proud of him. Then, we all sat on the field in the West end zone."

-Elizabeth Dunson

"I remember the 49ers final game in Kezar was tough. We lost to the Cowboys 17-10 in the 1970 NFC Championship Game. Two interceptions from quarterback John Brodie proved too much to overcome. For the next 18 years, Kezar stood mostly idle except for some high school football games. In 1989, the stadium suffered a great deal of damage in the earthquake which devastated much of the Bay Area. It was torn down, and reconstructed into a smaller venue. It doesn't look exactly as it once did, but Kezar remains a great tribute to the history of the area, and all of the great games played there."

-R. Terry

"One of the games I saw was against the Bears, the year after I got back from Vietnam. The second was against the Packers in '70. It was the game against the Packers, when I remember one play in particular. I was sitting in the Southwest corner of the stadium. The 49ers Bruce Taylor picked a pass at our 10-yard line near the North sideline. He ran to his left trying to outflank the coverage, but when he got to about the 15, he reversed his field and headed back to the other sideline. By this time, everyone was going nuts in the stadium, and there were bodies all over the field. He finally was gassed and someone either caught him from behind, or he tripped. But he had to have run 100 yards, and fell just short of the goal line. "

-Ken Delfino

"I remember the 1957 season at Kezar quite well. My husband and I had season tickets on the 35-yard line. We had to pull out four wins in five games with the alley-oop in the last two minutes to get as far as we did. To me, the mere threat of it was a great weapon, but reality is we won eight games, and tied for first. The playoff loss to the Lions was horrific, but the overall season was terrific."

-Heather Holmes

"We were season ticket holders 1968 and 1969. It was a very frustrating time for Niner fans. Although, we gave up our tickets before they made the playoffs in 1970, we were very frustrated with coach Dick Nolan and his play calling. He would have the 49ers run the ball 11 out of 14 times on first down with Ken Willard, a he-man behemoth on the field, and we'd end up giving-up the ball in the end. Nolan was a superb defensive coach, but we could predict almost every play when the Niners would run or pass, and so could the opponents. Nolan used to say how no one could stay one-on-one with Gene Washington or Clifton McNeil, but when they threw to them, it was usually third and eight, and the defense was ready. Back then, I promised my wife an exciting 49ers game. At each game she fell asleep."

-W. McGee

"It was a 1961 game against the Rams. Coach Hickey unleashed the 'shotgun' offense with Brodie, Kilmer and Waters - all playing quarterback. The 49ers won 35-0. I remember this game to this day, because of what happened before the game started, while the Rams were warming-up. I was sitting on the Northeast end right on the goal line. The Rams had drafted the McKeever brothers, Marlin and Mike, twins from USC. A lot of hype surrounded them, and their anticipated match-ups. Unfortunately for one of the twins, while tracking down a warm-up pass, the goal post got in his way. The posts were not located where they are today. One of the McKeever brothers ran full tilt into it. I can still hear the resounding crash of his helmet. He missed the game, and the 49ers dominated. Incidentally, both brothers died from head injuries years later."

-Alan Duncan

"My dad took me to my first 49ers game against the Rams in 1970. It was a rainy, miserable day, but the stadium was still pretty full. It was John Brodie vs. Roman Gabriel that day, and the Niners lost 30-13. I can still remember a couple of kids trying to watch the game for free by climbing up the base of the light towers just outside the stadium. Sitting on those hard, wooden bench seats wasn't very comfortable, but I was hooked. It was the last year of Kezar Stadium for pro football.

The Kezar Pub was formerly known as the famed Kezar Club

My last football game before they tore it down, was Saint Ignatius High vs. Sacred Heart High in 1982. I came back home from the Pacific Northwest last year, and took a walk around Bob St. Clair Field, before having lunch, and a drink at the Kezar Pub. Lots of good memories of that place."

-Michael Brock Alexander

"The 49ers weren't very good in the early days. I could be in constant state of euphoria or depression when the 49ers won or lost a game, because the of the long wait until next season. Yet, the last game of the 1965 season against the Packers would be special. Near the end of the game, my buddy and I went down on the field,. In those days Kezar didn't have a fence around the field, and kids could hop over the railing and get down on the field pretty easily. We were standing behind the Packers bench, and the best part was seeing Vince Lombardi up close. He was furious, and was yelling and swearing at his players. The game ended in a 24-24 tie. I was feeling too bad about the tie."

-Bob Ferretti

"The 1949 Niners-Colts game at Kezar left an indelible impression on me. Y.A. Tittle, who at the time played for the Colts, marched his team to the San Francisco goal line, where bodies collided and a Niner was helped to the sideline. Sitting in the end zone, I saw 49ers defensive end, Hal Shoener, point to a Baltimore player. The next play, a Colt was carried off the field. This was my first sense of the violent nature of football played at Kezar. The Colts folded after the 1950 season, and the 49ers added Tittle to their roster. It was a good move."

-Mario Basso

"I went to Kezar for a preseason game against the Eagles in 1953. What I remember most was the hit 49ers linebacker, Hardy Brown, put on Eagles running back, Troy Ledbetter. I knew about Brown, because I watched him at Oklahoma State. It was early in the game, and Ledbetter was carrying on a sweep to the right. Brown caught him with his shoulder, and the next thing I knew he was on the ground holding his head. The hit broke Ledbetter's cheekbone. It was the hardest hit I'd ever seen a 49er player give. Brown was an indiscriminate maimer. No one could figure out how he hit with the force he did. I remember Bears coach George Halas had officials check Brown's shoulder pads before a game. They found nothing. I had the opportunity to meet Brown after a game. He was reserved, but friendly, but on the field he was a killer."

-Jeffrey Anzalone

"When I played banjo in the 49ers band at Kezar, I never missed a performance. We were a rowdy bunch to say the least in our own right. At the games we wore black western hats, red shirts, an army cartridge belt (no guns) and leather boots. You could not watch a game without hearing the beat of our band. During one on-field brawl between the 49ers and Bears, a former pro-boxer, Charley Powell was duking it out in the end zone with a Bears player, and some of us band members jumped into the fray. We pulled our army belts off our pants and used them as weapons. None of us suffered any injuries. We usually had too much to drink anyway, but we had a wonderful time."

-Harold Means

"I would have been age eight in 1958, and remember my dad and I got all the way to the entrance to Kezar, before he realized he'd left our tickets at home. We lived in San Mateo, and went back, got them, came back and missed most of the first half. Once inside the stadium, I remember the bench seats were crammed in with my knees touching the fans in front of me. One of the most vivid memories was halftime entertainment, which featured a majorette by the name of Diane Nakamitsu. I remember how high her baton would go. She was performing the same role as band majorette at San Mateo High School, when I started there as a freshman in 1964."

-Michael Katz

"In 1949, I attended my first Niners game at Kezar. It just so happened my favorite star of screen and radio also showed for the game. I have vivid memories of Bob 'The Toe' Hope, exhibiting his rare skill, when he opened the halftime festivities by booting a kickoff a long twenty yards. The funny man was given a tremendous ovation for his antics and halftime discourse in front of a full house. Thanks Bob, for my favorite Kezar memory."

-Sandra Pluto

"I was there for the last game at Kezar played on January 3 1971, against the Dallas Cowboys for the NFC championship. Our seats were in Section KK. We lost a heart breaker 17-10. Later that year, Clint Eastwood filmed the famous 'Dirty Harry' scene at the stadium, where he shoots Scorpio from across the field. I was there too. My friend and I hid behind a trailer and made it into the stadium and walked into Kezar with the crew. I was surprised to see the white painted yard-lines were still visible on the field, probably left from the Dallas game."

-Ronald Drucker

"I grew up in the Parkside. In 1957, my dad purchased two 49er season tickets, which we kept in the family until the team moved to Santa Clara. My dad and my brother Bob went to the games together at Kezar. After one game my mother had a fit. The lady sitting behind Bob was not paying attention to the game, and burned a hole in his jacket with the tip of her cigarette. Mom was so furious."

-Ann Polacchi Jennings

"I only visited Kezar Stadium once, and what a thrill it was. 1954 to be exact. I was a member of the 95-piece marching band of Hollister High School. We entertained a full house, 59,000 49ers fans I'm told. When we played 'The 49ers Fight Song', the 49er fans let out a tremendous roar. The three-and-a-half-hour bus ride up Highway 101, and through the neighborhoods of San Francisco to the stadium was well worth it. It was a memory I'll never forget."

-Fred Roach

Kezar Concession Prices

Coca Cola	20-cents	Ice Cream	20-cents
Candy	10-cents	Cigarettes	35-cents
Hot Dog	25-cents	Cigars	10-cents
Beer	40-cents	Program	25-cents
Coffee	15-cents	Media Guide	25-cents
Lemonade	15 cents	Visor	10-cents
Peanuts	15-cents	Badge	25-cents
Popcorn	15-cents	Pennant	75-cents
Potato Chips	15-cents	Cap	$2.00

(1954 Harry M. Stevens Enterprises)

"I first saw Hardy Brown play, while watching the 1951 49ers vs Browns game at Kezar. Brown was a linebacker for the 49ers, best known for his 'shoulder tackles'. A Browns defensive back had just intercepted a pass by Frankie Albert and was weaving his way upfield, when a sudden movement on the field caught my eye. Then pow! It was like the flash fisherman might see in a stream before his line grows taut. As the Browns defender turned upfield, Brown struck him so violently with his shoulder in his face that his helmet popped up on his head and his back hit the ground before his feet. Standing over him was Brown. I could almost hear him chuckling. The stadium erupted. The following season I became a season ticket holder."

-Bruce Smith

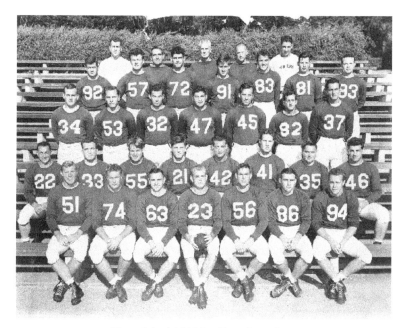

The original 1946 San Francisco 49ers

"I was at the 49ers first regular season game in 1946 - a 21-7 loss to the New York Yanks in front of 35,000 fans. The lowlight for Niners fans was the the heavier Yankee line manhandling of the 49ers, and rushing Albert off his feet. On Offense, Coach Flaherty's single-wing was unstoppable. A bright moment for me was in 1949, the Niners last AAFC game at Kezar - a playoff against the New York Yanks. This day Verle Lillywhite led a 49ers ground game that churned out 164 yards to help the Niners win 17-7, and advance to the AAFC title game."

-G. Richardson

"I'm 75 years old, but my first experience at Kezar was in December 1960, when I was in the stands for the showdown between the Packers and 49ers, both battling for a division crown. As a quintessential San Franciscan, I could hardly stand the pouring rain and brisk wind that greeted me that day. The favored 49ers could not move the ball against a stingy Packers defense on a muddy field, although most 49ers changed their cleats for better footing at halftime. I wanted to leave the game, but I stayed at the persuasion of my father, and froze until the game ended. The Packers went on to win 13-0, what became known as the 'Mud Bowl' at Kezar."

-Joe Muscarello

"It was November 17, 1968, and the 49ers were playing the Rams at Kezar. What a game it was! It was very close with the 1st quarter ending in a tie. By the end of the 2nd quarter the 49ers were in the lead by 3 points. The third quarter ended with neither team scoring a point and as the game wound down, the Rams would come from behind to win! A touchdown pass from Gabriel to Jack Snow! Awesome! But, suddenly a penalty negated their score. The Rams ended up kicking a field goal to tie the game. I would have loved to have seen them win, but they didn't lose. In all honesty, I was so thrilled to see them live. I would have still been happy if they had lost ... well, just maybe not quite as happy."

-Jim Fitzpatrick

"I was a 49ers Majorette, and performed at the home games at Kezar. Harry Belafonte signed my baton there. I was a really young majorette and moved around the stadium during the game and also with the Corps during halftime. We also went to pancake breakfasts with the 49ers before games. I remember Y.A. Tittle was there with the team."

-Janet Winans Kennedy

"I went to my first game in 1957. We were living in Truckee, about a three-hour drive to Kezar. I was eight. I went with my dad, and he bought me a 50-cent end zone ticket. I actually sat in the aisle, because I could not stand the smell of cigar smoke. We played the Rams and beat them 23-20. R.C. Owens made an alley-oop catch to beat them."

-Francine Stanish

Bears coach, George Halas is greeted by an unruly fan after a game

"I saw a game at Kezar vs the Bears. At the end of the game George Halas was running off the field, as a 49er fan stole his hat right off his head, we loved it. I'll always remember the mud games and the seagulls at the other end of the field. Oh, and those freeloaders across the street on the rooftops, and let's not forget the Kezar Club after the game."

-Denny Devins

"Around 1950, dad and I sat in the reserved section at Kezar. Sometime after the game started, more fans came over from the Christopher Milk section in mass groups towards the 50-yard line. This was more exciting for kids than the 'wave' is today."

-Lee Livingston

"During the '57 49ers - Lions playoff game loss, fans were jamming popsicle sticks in the mechanical time clock in the East end zone (a real 'Animal House') to stop the clock in the 4th quarter. It didn't matter, we lost the game anyway"

-Bill McDill

"We used to get in free at Kezar, and sneak in a case of beer. It was homey and local. The sad thing was watching the stadium decay. I played high school football inside the stadium, and at the 'Kezar Farewell' gathering in the '80s, before the wrecking balls came in, I brought my own football for autographs from 49er greats in attendance. There was Y.A. Tittle, R.C. Owens, Joe 'The Toe' Vetrano, Ted Kwalick, Abe Woodson, J.D. Smith and Leo 'The Lion' Nomellini, to name a few. Tittle said he missed Kezar, and remembered coming through the tunnel before they put the cage over it. He said he used to get doused with beer, sometimes while it was still in the bottle - and we were the home team! At the closing ceremony, I bought a cardboard number '10', which was used at the stadium's East scoreboard, and an eight-foot wood bench slab - both great memories from Kezar"

-Tom McDevitt

"I have bittersweet thoughts of Kezar. There were wooden benches with knees always in our backs. The best part though, was we could leave the stadium and go across the street to buy liquor and bring it back into the stadium. The roof tops were filled with fans watching the game, and I remember seeing players at the bars drinking heavy the night before a game at the Kezar Club."

-Shana McGrew

"My dad and my uncle were responsible for moving the equipment for the visiting teams into Kezar from 1946-52. Since my dad had field passes, I have fond memories of being on the field, and especially being given a football by John Henry Johnson, which I think I lost playing street football on Maynard Street in the city. I have dad's letters documenting pickup and delivery details for Kezar."

-Jim Flanigan

"My first date with the girl, who would later be my wife, was at a 49ers game in 1946. She became such a great fan over the years, until she passed away. She wore a 49er t-shirt in her coffin. My favorite Niners player was quarterback Frankie Albert, who later became our head coach. It is a shame he is not in the Hall of Fame. I had season tickets for many years. For the whole season it was $30. I remember many fans came from bars in the area, and were drunk by the time they got into the stadium. And boy, were they rowdy. Still Kezar was a grand place to watch games."

-Alfred Parodi

"I was raised a block away from Golden Gate Park in the Richmond District, so I used to walk to 49er games at Kezar. I served as an usher as a high schooler, which got me into games. My press box memories are as a working journalist. About half the press box was made-up with people other than the press. Early in my broadcast career, I became good friends with Hugh McElhenny, who was doing color commentary on 49ers radio broadcasts. We shared many tips and laughs. One of my fondest memories of Hugh was asking him about the persistent rumor regarding the way he wound up at the University of Washington, and not one of the Southern California schools. He said he followed a trail of ten-dollar bills. When I asked him again, he said, 'No, that's not true at all.' Then he paused, and said, 'They were twenties'."

-Barry Tompkins

"My mother and grandparents were regulars, and we've had season tickets in the family going back to Kezar. My grandparents were immigrants from Mexico, and always said 49ers tickets were their first real luxury."

-Peter Hartlaub

"During the '50s, if you ever hailed a vendor at Kezar, I was probably one of those who delivered hot dogs to you, with relish, a slab of mustard on a steamed bun. I was employed by Harry M. Stevens concessions company, who were in charge of all the concessions at Kezar. Stevens was a food concessionaire from England, who had been variously attributed as the inventor of the hot dog, and credited with being America's foremost ballpark concessionaire."

-Barry Rogoff

"When ordering food from a vendor at Kezar, he'd stop at the row where I was sitting. I would shout what I wanted to order, then pass down the money, which went from person to person to the vendor. My food was then passed back to me, but if there was any change from your purchase, it would mysteriously disappear."

-Nicholas Fairclough

"I first started going to 49ers games in 1964, as a 9-year old. My dad was an usher for the 49ers. He worked section OO and P, which was at the West end of Kezar. In the '60s, the 49ers were not very good and the crowds typically averaged 26,000 to 40,000. Since this was well below capacity, the 49ers allowed the ushers to bring their kids with them, and get into the game for free. We would sit in the bottom row of the section at field level. If we behaved ourselves, the 49ers were ok with this.

The ritual for going to the 49ers game were always the same. Be ready to leave the house by 10:00 a.m. on game day. Dad had to be outside Kezar by 11:00 a.m. to check-in and get his usher pass. My brother and I would then go over to the area leading to the locker rooms. There we would stand and watch buses pull-up, letting players off to walk the stairway down to the locker rooms.

We walked through the players' tunnel leading to the playing field, and onto the grass, until we reached our dad's section. We'd go down to the bottom row, and watch the pre-game activity. Usually, the 49ers band would be going through a practice run. Clementine, the mule also walked around the field with her guide. After awhile, the players would come out, and go through their warm-ups.

I enjoyed this as much as the game in those days, because I could see more of what was going on, as during the game our view was obstructed by players on the 49ers bench, especially when the game was taking place in the East end of the field. Doug Scofield, was our PA announcer, and for example would announce over the public address system, 'At flanker...from Bowling Green...#30...Bernie Casey', and the player would run out form the East end zone tunnel. We cheered for them all, as they came out.

At halftime, we would go up to meet dad, and go inside the stadium for some lunch. Dad would buy us hot dogs. He always referred to the hot dogs as 'Kezar steaks', so we always had 'steaks' with a cold drink, before going back to watch the second half.

At the end of the game, while walking back up the steps to meet dad, we would look through the rows until we found a program left behind. I'd bring it home to read from cover to cover."

-Tom Robertson

"Sometime during the '50s the 49ers were playing the Bears, and fans were riding 'Papa Bear' George Halas pretty good. There were a couple of guys behind me who called Halas every name in the book. Finally, as the game was nearing halftime, Halas turned around and looked at these guys and said something. A few minutes later the half came to an end and all the Bears ran off the field. Halas was walking behind them talking to an assistant. Suddenly one of the guys who had been doing all the yelling got out of his seat and headed towards the field toward Halas. From behind he kicked Halas right in the seat of his pants. Then he turned and ran back into the stands, before anyone could catch him. Halas turned around and didn't know what happened because the guy ran away so fast. It was one of the funniest things I've ever seen."

-Phil Butler

"I was 8-years old when I went to my first pro football game at Kezar with my father. I was a huge Packers fan, and was going to see my favorite team. My father bought a Packers pennant for me, and we proceeded into the stadium. Whenever the Packers would do something positive, I would wave that pennant and cheer. What I didn't realize was the home team fans didn't appreciate my pennant waving, and blocking their view of the game. My father had to calm a fan down, due to me restricting his view of the game. I was oblivious to the situation until he explained it to me later. John Brodie guided the 49ers to a victory. I was heartbroken and cried. My team had lost. Soon after, however, I often watched the 49ers, and have been a fan ever since. That was the only game at Kezar I ever saw, but am so thankful I went. My father and grandfathers went to a '47 game at Kezar. It was my father's first football game. So both myself and my father attended our first football games at Kezar."

-Scott Bezzo

"I think it was about 1966, and I was selling hot dogs. This was in the day when I had to put the hot dogs together with the bun and mustard. I had a container filled with hot water with the dogs in it, and on the side we kept the mustard and napkins. I was walking down the steps and the strap broke-off my shoulder holding the container. The whole thing tumbled down the steps with the mustard and large bills I kept under the container. Everything went flying! Some guy sitting about three rows down got spattered with mustard. It went all over his face, his cream-colored jacket and pants. I caught some heat from him, as well as from my boss. I lost about $20 - $30 in the accident."

-Bruce Lombardi

"While we should GO, GO, GO, GO!
We cheer the team of San Fran-cis-co,
While they GO, GO, GO, GO, GO!
Our gang shall drive and keep on roll-ing,
And across the goal they'll go.
Let's sing the For-ty Nin-ers' fight song,
While we shout GO, GO, GO, GO!"

The 49ers fight song by Martin Judnich debuted at Kezar on August 17, 1952

"I'm a 70-year old resident of San Francisco, who spent many seasons going to Kezar in the mid-1960s. At first we didn't have tickets, so we would find a way to sneak inside. One trick used was to wait for the ambulance to enter the stadium. They would open the huge gates at the West end zone, and we would crouch down behind the ambulance and follow it inside. Then run like hell! As we got older, we found out there was a cop at the nearby police station, who would give free tickets to the Christopher Milk section, about 30 minutes before game time. What we did for a few seasons was to get tickets, go to the section and wait 'til they played the National Anthem. Then we'd hop the fence and run to the better sections. After the game we would run on the field and ask the players for their chinstraps. We also took home a few footballs. Our best haul was when they were practicing field goals. We timed it just right, and ran on the field catching it mid-air before it reached the ball guy. Then we ran back to the stands, and left the stadium very quickly. Another time John Brodie was warming up, and the pass went off his receiver's shoulder pads, bouncing into the stands right where I was walking. Another ball to take home. After most games we would collect cushions, and get a nickel for each. With the money we made for the day, we would go to the park where the carousel was, and buy hot dogs for 20-cents apiece. It was like: go to the game with an empty pocket, and come home with some cash. Couldn't beat it."

-Dennis McCarthy

"My brother and I went to two games in 1970, the year Brodie won MVP, and the Niners went 10-3-1. We sat in the end zone bleachers for 50-cents. We packed lunches and saw them beat the Packers with Bart Starr, as well as the Colts under Johnny Unitas. As an 11-year old fan seeing his first pro games live with legends to boot, it was wonderful. And yes, the bleachers were incredibly rowdy."

-Jeffery McKinnon

"I was 10 years old in 1955, when I became a 49ers fan for life. My parents were farmworkers, and we lived in humble beginnings. I had a simple hobby of collecting 5-cent packs of football cards. I recall my first card was a rookie card of 49ers Dicky Moegle. Not sure why, but I instantly became a 49ers fan living in Fresno. All my friends were Rams fans, and I took a lot of ribbing. As a poor kid, I knew I would never afford to go to Kezar, yet my childhood 'impossible dream' was to see the 49ers play in San Francisco.

I got married in 1970, and we drove to San Francisco for our honeymoon. I recall waking up early Sunday morning, and just casually reading the Sporting Green. I was surprised to see the 49ers had a home game against the Denver Broncos. My 49er excitement had reawakened. I asked my wife if she wanted to go to the game. She agreed. We jumped in our car, and drove quickly to Kezar. Our quarterback, John Brodie threw a 61-yard TD pass to rookie John Isenbarger to defeat the Broncos 19-14. A month later I came to the realization that my childhood dream had come true. What a lasting, unforgettable experience it was to see a game at Kezar."

   -Angel Perea

"I went to Kezar with my dad, uncle and other family members to watch the Niners. We took the N street car, and I saw Y.A. Tittle, Gale Sayers, Gene Washington, Leo Nomellini and others. I have some game programs from Kezar in my hope chest. One time my mom was pregnant with my sister in 1968. My brother used my dad's ticket to the Niners game on November 3, 1968. The family joke was my dad missed the Browns - Niners game to be with my mother for the birth of my sister. I gave the program from that game to my sister as a gift."

   -Linda Alio Wendt

"I was a 49ers ball boy in 1956, and have many memories being on the sidelines with the players. I had this golfer's portable chair I'd carry around for coach Albert everywhere he went. It was the kind you unfold and stick in the turf. At practices and home games at Kezar he used it."

-Paul Dastageer

"In 1966, my friend Vic and I decided to ride to the 49ers - Lions game with my grandfather and his friends. We were going to pay for General Admission tickets, yet while in line to purchase tickets, a guy approached us wanting to know if we would like to get in the game for free. Vic and l looked around, and saw there was a policeman standing close by, but we still went over to talk to this guy. It turns out he and his buddy were photographers, and they wanted us to carry their cameras on the sidelines. Neil and Walter were their names. They even gave us $20 at halftime to spend on lunch. We forgot to give them the change. I waved to my grandfather from the field, but he didn't see us. Vic and I had the press passes to prove to my grandfather we were on the field that day. It wasn't until years later that I found out we had worked with Neil Liefer and Walter Iooss Jr. from 'Sports Illustrated.' I will never forget that day and the experience of a lifetime."

-Kevin Richardson

"I was dating my husband, and he bought me a nice warm coat to wear to 49ers games, as we went almost every Sunday. What I remember most was fog rolling in, and seagulls flying over and picking up food. I was so afraid that we would get pooped-on, I put a newspaper over my head. I didn't understand the game much, but I loved going to Kezar. Fun times."

-Clarice Keane Watson

"I have vivid memories of two particular games against the Bills and Yanks in 1948. I was working the sidelines as a photographer, when holy criminy, Joe Perry, a rookie ran for a 58-yard touchdown the very first time he carried the ball. I tried to get a closeup of coach Shaw screaming in a frenzy, but was shoved away. During the next game against the Yanks, it was near impossible to take photos, as over 60,000 fans stormed Kezar. Because of fire regulations, they turned away thousands more wanting to get in. Fans were standing on the track, constantly bumping or running into me. It's the way it was at wild and woolly Kezar."

-Gus Leviticus

"I remained faithful to the 49ers in fair times and foul. When my cousin and I attended games at Kezar in 1963, they fell into the dumps, going 2-12. The number of no-shows at Kezar was alarming. The best part was we could move around the stadium for better seats. Also, it seemed the team cut off relations with the public. I remember calling the Niners office for something free for my son, like a pocket schedule, but they never returned my call. That year was the last time we saw a game at Kezar."

   -Bucky Walter

"Going to Kezar was a big deal for my friends and me in the '60s. But one thing bothered me at the stadium. Before each game, Dave Scofield, the 49ers PA announcer, introduced only the offensive or defensive team lineups. I felt the entire team deserved recognition and applause from the fans. This oversight could have been remedied if Scofield, when the starters took the field, would have said, 'and the rest of the 49ers players and coaching staff'. I'll admit, this was a small suggestion, but wish I had said something back then."

   -Bob Liston

"Kezar was a rickety, dated stadium nestled among the tall oak trees at the Southeast part of Golden Gate Park. 49ers players and visitor alike dreaded the close proximity of rowdy fans, all juiced-up from their pregame rituals in nearby bars. The locker rooms appeared to have been built in another century. Seagull droppings proved to be a constant hazard for unsuspecting fans and players. Although Kezar will be remembered as an antiquated, neighborhood stadium in the middle of town, it was a site of countless, priceless memories in the heart of San Francisco 49ers lore."

   -Bruce Jenkins

"I was a member of the original 'Goal Rushers Booster's Club' in 1953. At first we had 1,000 members, and by the end of the decade there were eight chapters and 3,200 members. We held weekly meetings at the Fairmont Hotel, and on Sundays, many of us took chartered buses to Kezar. Our tickets were in section MM. After games we would meet at the Kezar Club, a watering hole on Stanyan, directly across the street from Kezar. The place was decorated in warm reds and golds, and almost always packed with 49ers players. What a ball we had!"

-Liz O'Mara

"They talk about the 'friendly confines' of Wrigley Field. Well, Kezar wasn't so friendly, but the confines were very similar. You could almost touch the players, and see their expressions. Kezar was a neighborhood stadium, the kind no NFL team could build today given infrastructure demands and real estate costs. It was just blocks from the corner of Haight and Ashbury, which surely made for strange bedfellows when the 'Summer of Love' coincided with the 1967 season."

-Lon Simmons

"I was age 12 when my dad, his buddy Bob and I went to kezar for the Rams game. Bob was a classic jerk, always with the wise cracks. Still I loved the guy. Late in the game, the 49ers were listless, and the Rams were way ahead and utterly dominant. Jon Arnett was running wild for the Rams. Well, Bob could no longer contain himself. He'd seen enough. Red faced, veins bulging out of his forehead, he stood up and yelled, 'God damn you Rams! I hope the seagull's shit on you!'. In that very instance, Bob was strafed by a seagull, and white bird crap splattered on top of his head. Without missing a beat, he raised his arms in resignation, looked to the sky and said, 'Ask and ye shall receive'.

-George DiChristina

"I worked as one of the teams' statisticians in the Kezar press box from 1950 until 1954. I recall Bud Foster, Roy Story and Lon Simmons did the radio broadcasting and Bob Fouts did the TV commentaries. KPIX televised the 49ers games in black and white, but all home games were blacked out within a 150-mile radius. Tony and Vic Morabito sat just one row down from me. We all had a great time and great snacks too. What I remember most was the '54 season when the 49ers won their first 11 games. Six were preseason games, and five were league games, which included a tie to open the season. Then Y.A., McElhenny and Perry got hurt. We ended up 7-4-1."

-Harry Sorenson

"I first went to Kezar in the late '50s, and learned the art of seating migration. A friend of my dad's was a ticket taker, and a few of us would each hand him a candy wrapper, saving us about $4.00 each - or three-hour's worth of my paycheck from Playland at the Beach. Then we'd head for the West end zone, where there were always empty seats. From there, we'd migrate slowly through the crowds, often making it to the 40-yard line by halftime."

-J. Burch

"After the 1957 season, there were so many unhappy wails from fans, who purchased season tickets at Kezar, and were not able to improve their locations. There were only 19,000 seats between the goal lines. Once we considered adding backs to the wooden benches, but it would have brought down the 59,000 capacity to 35,000. We scratched that idea. Several times I was forced to referee for divorcing couples, who claimed custody of choice seats."

-Peter Giannini

"The original Kezar was really a fun place for a 49ers football game. Yep, the streetcars and buses used to run well enough to get people to and from the stadium. People got off buses and out of cars, or walked from the bars and grills that used to line Haight and Lincoln Way. Kezar wasn't fancy or manicured. It was, however, wide-open and boisterous. Everyone had a good time. And, it seems after every losing season we could hear the chant from fans ... 'Wait 'til next year!' That phrase became a ritual year after year."

-Jerry Fyne

"I remember what a dark day it was for my brother and I after we saw our 49ers lose 31-27 to Detroit in the '57 playoff game. We stayed around after the game to greet the 49ers players with our condolences. We spoke briefly with 49er Joe Arenas. I said, 'Sorry Joe'. He replied, 'That's the way it goes sometimes', and boarded the bus. The killer was when a huge Detroit lineman emerged smoking a big cigar and yelled to the crowd with a big laugh, 'What do you think of us now folks?'"

-Paul Laveroni

"My best friend and I lived on 3rd and Hugo, about three blocks from Kezar. In the '50s, when the 49ers played on Sundays, parking was limited, so we would charge $1.50 a car to use our driveways. The $1.50 got us two end zone seats for being under 12-years old. We would put our hair in pigtails, and managed to pass as under 12, 'til we were 16. The best part of those days was waiting after games in the parking lot for the players to come out. We had favorites like Bob St. Clair, and both of us had a crush on Dicky Moegle. Our favorite by far was Bruce Bosley, and his beautiful wife Barbara.

I can't remember how it developed, but somehow we convinced other kids Bruce was our uncle. He'd often leave us tickets at will-call - 30-yard line, or better. To make a long story short, he was the nicest man, and a hell of a ball player, who went along with two starstruck, teenage girls.

It was a special time in professional football for the 49ers, and the simple time we lived growing up so close to Kezar. When Bosley passed away, I cried for the sweet gentle man, who played great football and supported two girls' fantasies. I remember my friend calling and telling me 'Uncle Bruce passed'."

-Suzan Riddell

"I grew up in Sacramento in the '60s, and went to quite a few games at Kezar. One overcast Sunday it was drizzling, and the Packers were in town. One play, Paul Hornung ran around end, and flew head first into the end zone, sliding 10-yards on his belly. The skid marks remained there the whole game. I remember how cramped we were sitting on those wood benches. Our seats were high in the end zone, and just behind us were two sailors in uniforms drinking beers and bourbon. By the third quarter, they were passed out. It seemed there were always distractions, but we loved going to the games."

-Ron Fritzsche

"My dad worked as a ticket taker at Kezar for years. After games he would go over to an office by the police station to count money and balance receipts. I remember helping him a few times with this. We'd talk about all the violence at the 49ers games, especially during the team's pioneering first years at the stadium. I saw the 49ers play in their debut years after World War II, and sold programs during the early '50s, which was a very good deal. I'd make $5 or so, and get to see the game for free. Sometimes a fist fight, usually a brief one marked by salvos of beer, was thrown-in. The last game at Kezar, when Dallas beat the Niners, 17-10, for the NFC Championship, I saw 20+ young men in a post-game rampage toss bottles and cans at the crowd. Thirteen people were treated for cuts and bruises, and 22 arrests were made. While my most vivid memories of violence at Kezar is still with me, I loved Kezar for its passionate and sometime outlandish fans, it was a true throwback stadium."

-James O. Clifford, Sr

"My first trip to San Francisco I came to take-in my hometown heroes at Kezar Stadium, where Lions players had mentioned they loved playing. The Lions were victorious over the Niners 26-17. Not only was I impressed by the mild weather and the hot dogs at Kezar, but after the game I met my idol, Alex Karras, and my neighbor from Lansing, MI, Roger Brown. I said, 'Hello' to Mr. Brown. 'I'm Don your neighbor from Pennington Avenue, and it's nice to meet you Mrs. Brown'. Well, Brown gave me the dirtiest look you could ever imagine. The lesson I learned was obvious. This was not Mrs. Brown. I decided not to attend any more Lions games. Ironically, we moved to the Bay Area permanently five-years later, and soon after I became a huge 49ers fan. Kezar became my second home."

-Don Surath

"I was a Colts fan attending Niner games at Kezar. I grew up in Landover, MD, and my job as a chemical engineer brought me to the Bay Area. I remember the Colts and Niners were battling for a Western Division title in '57, and the game was a sellout. The day before I watched the Colts practicing near Children's Playground in the park. I recall Unitas and Berry after practice working on pass routes until near darkness, while the other players waited in the bus. The game was a classic. A see-saw battle, but when it seemed my Colts would win the game, Brodie teamed up with McElhenny to beat us 17-13. In the game a Niners rookie, Jerry Mertens, caught my attention. He covered our fleet Lenny Moore, Unitas's deep threat, and Mertens shut him down the whole game. Afterwards, our coach Eubank filled his Pro Bowl roster by adding Mertens to the squad. The whole scenario was pretty exciting."

-Sal Santore

"Going to the games with dad were the best of times. In the '60s I was a big Brodie fan, but also a fan of Bart Starr of the Packers. On December 1, 1968, we were both excited to go to Kezar for the Packers - 49ers game. I remember how disappointed I was when Starr did not start the game, as he was nursing a shoulder injury. Instead, his back-up Bratkowski played poorly, and was pulled from the game. Ultimately, Starr got his chance late in the game, but my excitement was short lived, as Brodie was terrific and rallied the 49ers to beat Green Bay, 27-20. After the game I squeezed my way between a small crowd at my dad's urging to get a glimpse of my hero by the player's dressing rooms. There he was, No. 15 emerging from the shadows of a tunnel. He briefly looked up at me, giving a heads-up gesture and made his way towards the visitor's dressing room. What happened next was the topper of disappointments for me. Someone booed Starr, and threw trash at him."

-Tom Walsh

"I sold programs at Kezar during the 1947 and '48 seasons. I'm 87 now, and my memory is somewhat faulty. However, what is still vivid, are the sights and sounds of two 'bull-elephant' players colliding on the 20-yard line at the West end of Kezar. The players were the Niners Norm Standlee, and the Browns Marion Motley. In those days our boys played both ways on offense and defense. Both were fullbacks and both played linebacker on their respective teams. Well Standlee, playing offense hit Motley straight on, and both ended up unconscious. I was bug-eyed, sitting low in the stands seeing and hearing the collision. Both players resumed playing a short while after - an event I'll never forget."

-Leo Koulos

"In 1954, I was fortunate to see my dad, Burt Delevan, play against the 49ers at Kezar. At the time he was serving in the Army. There was no pampering of the Fort Ord athletes, as the 49ers beat them 42-14. But, the highlight of my day was watching dad help score a touchdown for the Army. Jimmy Powers was the Army quarterback. In the fourth quarter his desperation pass was batted away by a 49er. Dad, who was playing defensive tackle, caught it, but could not hold it, so he knocked it backwards into the hands of Ernie Brodier, who lateraled it to halfback Dave Mann, who ran it in for a touchdown. Dad said later he knew he was an ineligible receiver, and did the right thing to avoid a penalty."

-Barry Delevan

6

Brawlers

"I believe it was the 1954 49ers season at Kezar, and I was in the seventh grade at Presidio Jr. High. I'm at a 49er game with my brother, and these bunch of drunks have a Coleman cooler full of beer. They went obnoxious and spilled beer everywhere. They were part of the hooligans and youngsters who tried to rip down a goal post, but they were unsuccessful, and were attacked by the police. My brother and I were just happy to get out of the stadium alive. The next day, our school said there would be a special assembly for boys, and a uniformed SFPD officer said he compared the riot at Kezar to VJ Day. In spite of the rioters - mostly drunk adults, the officer told us if something like that happens again, they wouldn't allow any youngster in Kezar."

-Brad Fennison

"Kezar had 59,000 seats, only 15-inches wide, and only 20-inches separated the back of a fan from the knees of the guy in the row behind. Kezar was full of unruly fans. There was a lot of beer drinking, and also the hard stuff. There were a lot of fights - everyone who went to a 49ers game remembers them. The crowd was more blue-collar then, and most of the people in the stands were mechanics, teamsters, and waterfront workers on their day off. Tough guys. That was our fan base. But not everybody was blue-collar. A friend told me about one game he went to with a prominent surgeon. The surgeon brought a big pitcher of martinis, and proceeded to drink it all during the game. Someone sitting nearby said something he didn't like, and the surgeon threw the pitcher at the guy and it hit him right in the head. Of course, a fight ensued between them. Team president, Lou Spadia called it 'human nature'. It certainly wasn't 'Downton Abbey!'"

-Carl Nolte

"It was one of those rare hot Sundays in the city, and the 49ers were playing the Rams in 1969. From the West tunnel, the 49ers Majorettes came marching out, preceded by the 49ers band. They headed to the other end of the stadium, where players waited to be introduced. Prior to the kickoff, the Armed Forces color guard came marching out. They looked great in their dress uniforms with polished chrome helmets and white gloves. After the National Anthem, they marched toward the West end zone, as someone threw a beer bottle from the stands towards the color guard. He missed. The security quickly escorted this guy out of the game. I wasn't too surprised, as there was a lot of protesting going on relating to the Vietnam War. Still, most of the fans were patriotic. They applauded the color guard, as they passed us in the West end zone."

-Harold Christensen

"I saw many games at Kezar. Once I saw this drunk person behind me throw a bottle and hit a referee on the field. I couldn't believe it. I was sitting in the West end zone with my father in the middle of the Grambling college marching band. The drunk who threw the bottle was grabbed by many band members, who turned him over to security."

Bob Hatch

Hugh McElhenny (left) is attacked by a flock of Eagles

"One of my most vivid memories of Kezar Stadium is from my very first 49ers game. It was September 1953, the first game of the season. The 49ers were playing the Eagles. My father and I were sitting high up near the West end zone. Being only nine-years old, I didn't know much about football at the time, although my father did his best to explain the rules to me. While I do not remember the scoring or any particular plays, I certainly do remember the donnybrook which broke out on the field. I remember two Eagles players chasing a zig-zagging Hugh McElhenny toward the West end zone. Before long, the 49ers band stormed onto the field to ward off the Eagles and protect Hugh. All over the field, fights were erupting. Soon, fans were pouring from the stand to join in the fracas, and mounted police were on the field trying to get things under control. In 1997, I met Y.A. Tittle at a restaurant, and we discussed that game. Y.A., who was quarterback for the 49ers then, stated the melee was perhaps the wildest one in the history of the league."

-Phil Lichtenstein

"It was 1958, and I was sitting in section MM at Kezar when this 49er fan jumped over the railing and rushed onto the field. He took a swing at the Bears head coach, George Halas. A group of Bears assistants pulled the fan away from him, and got their own licks in. The guy was taken away in a paddy wagon and the fans cheered. The Bears won the game 27-14, but we enjoyed the brawl."

-Al Levy

"The last game at Kezar was a donnybrook. First, we lost to the Cowboys 17-10 in the NFC playoffs. Then all hell broke loose. In fact, the players had left the field, when a riot broke loose in the West end zone. Luckily, my brother and I had seats on the 20-yard line away from the melee. It looked like about 50 thugs went on a rampage fighting each other, kicking people, dumping them in the aisles. They were throwing ice cubes, whiskey bottles, beer cans - even a water cooler. We don't know if it was camaraderie or disgust that started it. To me, it seemed like an appropriate way to close an era where drunkenness and brawling had been a familiar aspect of Kezar since the 49ers started playing there."

-Mark Borenstein

"On a cold Sunday in 1964, my mom took my brother and me to a game at Kezar vs the Bears. Two Bears fans behind us were drinking Jack Daniel's, while shouting 'Go Bears!'. By halftime, the bottle of liquor was drained. During the third quarter, one of those two drunks got sick, and vomited all over me. My mother was furious, and gave them a lecture. I was so thrilled to be in the city and have gone to the game, but it was bittersweet, because of the incident. My mom complained to 49ers management, who sent us a letter of apology, and a stack of player photos.

-Ronald Longinotti

"I grew up in the Sunset District in the city, born exactly two weeks after the Niners were founded. I took my girl friend to the 1966 game against the Packers. We were sitting in the end zone when Packers quarterback, Bart Starr, got ko'd by the 49ers pass rush. They carried him off the field on a stretcher through the middle of the end zone by the tunnel. The passage had a cyclone fence on the top and sides to the entrance. To my surprise, unruly fans drenched Starr with beer, as he laid half unconscious. Kezar fans were just lawless in those days."

-Carl Janson

SAN FRANCISCO
FORTY NINERS

1255 POST STREET · SAN FRANCISCO, CALIFORNIA 94109 · PRospect 1

January 11, 1967

Mrs. Eugene Longinotti
20 Santa Maria Lane
Hillsborough, California 94010

Dear Mrs. Longinotti:

Mr. Giannini has given me your letter of 7 January and I certainly am sorry for the unpleasantness you incurred at the stadium during the season.

We would be more than happy to move you away from that location if you so desired.

Perhaps we cannot totally erase your son's disillusionment, but may be the enclosed may in some measure indicate our concern for the maltreatment and abuse he sustained.

My personal best wishes for the New Year.

Cordially,

Art Johnson
Asst. Gen. Mgr.

Encl.

Kezar Artifacts

Forty Niners

KEZAR STADIUM EVENT PARKING

VIPS . PRESS . TV . RADIO . FIELD
PHOTOGRAPHERS . EMPLOYEES
MUST SHOW CREDENTIALS

NO RV's or Campers
NO Overnight Camping
NO Loitering-Police Enforced!
NO Parking in Fire Lanes
(PARK CODE SECTION 3.13)

UNAUTHORIZED VEHICLES SUBJECT TO TOWING
(PARK CODE SECTION 703 U)

FOR TOWED VEHICLES CALL Overland 1-2691

OPERATED BY RECREATION & PARKS DEPARTMENT - 1955 SAN FRANCISCO 49ers FOOTBALL CLUB

FOOTBALL
- TODAY -
KEZAR STADIUM
THIS CAR DIRECT
VIA
SHORTEST ROUTE

HAVING EXACT FARE
IS YOUR HELP
FOR A FASTER RIDE

MUNICIPAL RAILWAY SF

Forty Niners

TICKETS FOR SALE

ALL GAMES KICKOFF AT 1:00 PM

RESERVED SEATS............$3.75
GENERAL ADMISSION.....$3.00
(SECTION P-00 W CC D ONLY)
GENERAL ADMISSION.....$2.00
WHEN RESERVED............$2.50
(END ZONE ONLY)
CHILDREN UNDER 12..... .50¢
(EAST END ZONE ONLY)
JUNIOR 49ERS-CLUB ENTER GATE 21

KEZAR STADIUM STRICTLY PROHIBITS:
GUNS . DOGS . THROWING OF BEER BOTTLES .
DRUNK OR DISORDERLY FANS . ENTERING THE PLAYING FIELD
VIOLATORS WILL BE SUBJECT TO EJECTION
FROM STADIUM WITHOUT A REFUND

© 1955 SAN FRANCISCO RECREATION AND PARKS DEPARTMENT

SAN FRANCISCO
KEZAR STADIUM

CHICAGO BEARS
vs.
Forty Niners

ENTER GATE 11A ONLY

SUNDAY, NOVEMBER 19, 1961
KICKOFF 1:30 P.M.

EMPLOYEE

N⁰   68

- FOOTBALL -
LOS ANGELES RAMS
vs. SAN FRANCISCO FORTY-NINERS
- KEZAR STADIUM -
SUNDAY, NOVEMBER 29, 1970 - 1:00 P.M.
CHILD UNDER 12
ADMISSION 50¢

0633

49ERS
GATEMAN
14

It's NOT too LATE

ORDER YOUR SEASON TICKETS NOW

Still Available

- Season tickets guarantee you a choice seat for every game, as well as an option to your seat year after year.
- They are an excellent means by which to entertain your friends and business associates. More and more firms are purchasing season tickets for customer entertainment.

See Them All

1952 TICKET PRICES

SEASON TICKET PRICES		SINGLE GAME PRICES
$22.50		$3.75
$18.00		$3.00

End Zone — When General Admis...
When Reserved . .

Season Ticket Sale Closes September 16th

SAN FRANCISCO FORTY NINERS
SEASON TICKET ORDER - 1952

Name

Address

SAN FRANCISCO *Forty Niners*

1957 SEASON TICKET

seats will be assigned as close to section requested as possible

My check or money order for $_____ (add $.30 for (insurance) is enclosed herewith.

MAKE CHECKS PAYABLE to SAN FRANCISCO FORTY NINERS
Room 425 · 760 Market Street · DO. 2-7969

JR.49er MINOR CLUB

ENTER GATE A

RESERVED SEATS ONLY
GENERAL ADMISSION SEATS

→

KEZAR STADIUM

★ FORT ORD ★
VS.
S.F. 49ers
SUNDAY, AUG. 8th, 1954
KEZAR STADIUM, S. F.
SPONSORED BY THE SAN FRANCISCO
CALL-BULLETIN
MILITARY PAGEANT & SPECTACULAR RALLY STUNTS!
Reserved Seats $3.75 & $2.50 Service Men .50¢
for the Benefit of the Christmas Fund & Army Athletic & Recreation Funds

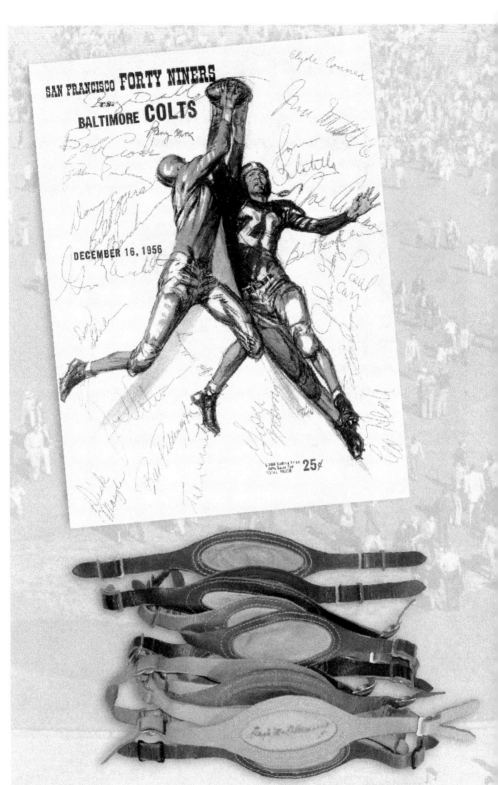

The DIGGINGS

SAN FRANCISCO FORTY NINERS

JUNE, 1969

LOMBARDI, REDSKINS OPEN 49er HOME SEASON

Falcons, Packers Are First Road Opponents

1946 Season
INFORMATION BOOKLET
★
SAN FRANCISCO

Forty Niners

ALL AMERICA FOOTBALL CONFERENCE

SAN FRANCISCO FORTY NINERS

Press Box Telephone

FOR RESERVATIONS
INFORMATION, STORIES,
PICTURES OR MATS, WRITE

PUBLICITY DEPARTMENT,
THE FORTY NINERS
212 STOCKTON STREET
SAN FRANCISCO, 8

1950 SCHEDULE

San Francisco
49'ers

Broadcast again by
ACME BEER

7

Owners, Coaches, Players

"After a night at the Holiday Inn, we took two buses to Kezar. One bus was the 'Good Apple' bus with coaches and players who didn't drink beer. The 'Bad Apple' bus would stop for six-packs and salami. After games our head coach always had beer for his players. Our first few games were not broadcast at the start of the season. When the season was a couple of games old, we came up with a sponsor, Tarantino's Restaurant on Fisherman's Wharf. In the pre-television era, fans listened to games, and created their own images of the players. Soon after, 49ers fans started coming to the games to see how their images corresponded to reality. That's the way it was."

-Al Sorrell

"In 1946, I was the 49ers ticket and equipment manager. For our first league game against the New York Yankees at Kezar, we had around 1,400 advanced season ticket sales. The prices were $3.60 and $2.40 for reserved seats and $1.20 for general admission. I hired 14 ticket takers for the game. It was a beautiful day, and 60,000 - maybe more showed up. Suddenly I needed another 28 ticket takers. I became one of them. We were totally unprepared. God knows how many got into the game using streetcar transfers, and made-up stuff. There were people writing checks, and handing them to the gate men. It was total chaos. There were people sitting on the track. We made a lot of changes in the future."

-Lou Spadia

"I was stationed at Ft. Ord Army Training Center in 1954, and under contract with the Niners, as was our quarterback Jimmy Powers. We were thrilled to find out we would be returning to Kezar Stadium, but as Fort Ord Warriors, in a game against my 49er teammates. Our fullback, Ollie Matson, a native San Franciscan, was just as excited as we were. The week before we lost to the Rams 7-0, so we expected a close game in San Francisco. The base chartered a dozen buses full of soldiers to support us. Only about 20,000 showed up at Kezar, but it was an epic moment for all of us. We lost 42-14, but personally, I played a damn good game. I played offensive and defensive end, and linebacker that day. I didn't catch a pass, but on defense I dropped Billy Tidwell for an 11-yard loss, and sacked Y.A. I forced a Pete Schabarum fumble. It was such a thrill to be back on the same field with my buddies."

-Ed Henke

MORABITO DIES AT 49ER GAME
Team Rallies to 'Win for Tony'

San Francisco Chronicle **FINAL**
THE VOICE OF THE WEST

MONDAY, OCTOBER 28, 1957

'A Win for Tony'

49er Owner Dies
At Kezar After
Heart Attack

Death in the Stadium

Mystery
Of Zhukov
Deepens

The Chronicle
Recommends:

"October 27, 1957, was a heartfelt moment for me and the 49ers organization. The Bears were in town, the weather wasn't very good. Team owner Tony Morabito, sitting in the press box, said, 'we had to win this game for the fans'. Beginning the second half, with the Bears leading us 17-7, Tony suddenly slumped over in his chair. He had suffered another heart attack, (The first one was in 1952), but this one was his final installment. Dr. Frank Cox immediately began applying artificial respiration, while I sent someone down to the field to find Dr. Bill O'Grady, our team's physician. Tony was rushed to St. Mary's Hospital. Neither the fans at the stadium nor the radio audience knew Tony had been stricken. When a note 'Tony's gone' was passed to coach Albert on the field in the middle of the third quarter, the 49ers stormed back for a 21-17 upset victory."

-Franklin Mieuli

"I had terrible vision, and wasn't going to wear glasses. There was a giant scoreboard clock at the East end of Kezar. Like other aging stadiums, it had a minute and a second hand, denoting how much time was left in a quarter. And when those old clocks wound down to the final minute, with two hands converging, I had difficulty determining how much time remained in a quarter. Of course, I had Frankie Albert with his eyes on the field which helped."

-Lawrence "Buck" Shaw

"I especially remember one emotional game against our archrival LA Rams at Kezar in 1951. We walloped them 44-17. I played nose-guard during the game, and had been gobbling up the Rams quarterback, Norm Van Brocklin, all afternoon. We tussled, spat at each other, and he got angry as hell. Then right there in the middle of the game, he makes a pledge to me, to meet him in the Kezar tunnel after the game to settle the score. Well, after the game I was still boiling from emotions, I waited for him in the tunnel. Finally he shows up. I was ready to rumble, but he diffused the situation. He even said 'wanna grab a beer?'. In the end, I really don't think he wanted to see me again."

-Visco Grgich

"Playing ball at Kezar made me proud to be a 49er. I attended Poly HIgh across the street from the stadium, and played all my high school games there. And to think my football career started there, and I kept thinking my football career would probably end right there where it began - at Stanyan and Frederick Streets. Frankie Albert threw a lot of passes my way, and I was the happiest guy that ever put a cleat on the Kezar turf."

-Alyn Beals

"My first love was the 49ers, and I ushered at Kezar, beginning as a 17-year old high schooler. My job was to point people to their seats, but it was basically just a way to get to watch the 49ers for free. When I was not working the games, I found other ways to watch. I was on the roof of a classmate's house on Frederick Street adjacent to Kezar, when R.C. Owens made his first alley-oop catch. What I saw at Kezar throughout the years, wasn't exactly championship football. After the playoff loss

to the Lions in '57, gloom and doom hung over the city. One of the most astonishing, impossible catches ever wrought on any gridiron was made at Kezar by rookie receiver R.C. Owens in 1957, a 23-20 win against the Rams. He went in the air like a tightly coiled spring, and held onto the ball. The 49ers walked out of the jungle proud victors."

-George Seifert

KEZAR STADIUM

"San Francisco has always been my favorite booing city. I don't mean the people boo louder or longer, but there is a special intimacy. When they boo you, you know they mean you. Music, that's what it is to me. One time at Kezar they gave me a standing boo. I felt honored."

-George Halas

"Reflecting on Kezar Stadium is easy for me, because there was no other stadium where I played, and was so embraced by it's fans. My fondest memory of Kezar happened in my first game as a 49er in 1951. All rookies - about 10 of us - learned a lesson in spirit and desire to win. The team was so passionate about the game, and supported us to the fullest with their enthusiasm. That season we played the 1950 World Champion Cleveland Browns in our first home league game at Kezar. Instead of folding against the world champs, we beat them handily 24-10. That game was probably my most gratifying game as a pro."

-Pete Schabarum

"At first, I worked in the scoreboard shack at the East end of the stadium. We did everything manually with numbered cards, and wore headsets, conversing with the referees on the field. To say that job was hectic would be an understatement, as sometimes we unintentionally mixed up the cards, and put up an '8' instead of maybe a '4'. After we heard the crowd roar, we looked through a small window. Someone would shout back we put up the wrong number. We didn't get paid much in those days, but I did get free hot dogs.

Kezar's notorious East end zone, and scoreboard

Later, I was a freshman at Menlo Jr. College where the 49ers practiced, and a 49ers ball boy. One night there was a small fire near the 49ers locker room. I reported it, and got a rewarded $100 from Lou Spadia. Another time, I was called in an emergency before the season-ending home game with the Yankees. Our kicker, Joe Vetrano, had left his kicking shoes back at Menlo JC. With kickoff approaching, I was assigned to fetch them, and borrowed 49ers end, Hal Shoener's big Lincoln Continental convertible. It took 35-40 minutes. Joe Perry had filled-in for kicking duties until Joe made it back to the stadium."

-Ken Flower

"It was the worst stadium in the league. The locker rooms were built for high school teams. It was horrendous really. It was also cramped. Many of the worst seats in the stadium were located in the first twelve rows. Many players were within earshot of fans hurling verbal jabs at them, and well within range of the garbage that was occasionally thrown. We just became accustomed to it. As with any stadium, there were many unique moments and games which took place at Kezar."

-Joe Perry

"What was Kezar like? If you're losing and coming out of the long tunnel, it was like the Roman Coliseum. The slaves coming out to be fed to the lions, and people up there cheering. It was real dusty too in the tunnel. We always tried to be the first team out, and we'd kick up the dirt. We wanted to make it as uncomfortable as possible for the visitors. You could hear the other team behind us coughing and gasping."

-Y.A. Tittle

"Kezar Stadium was a wonderful place to play. The playing surface was usually a wreck by the time we played on it, as all of the high schools in the city would play there. By November, the field got all torn up between the hash marks on the dirt. I do have one regret. I would have liked to kick more field goals at Kezar, but coach Buck Shaw didn't believe in field goals. He believed in touchdowns. No matter where we were on fourth down – even if we were in field goal range, he was going for the first down."

-Gordy Soltau

"I loved Kezar. I really felt I belonged. Maybe 100 fans or so would greet me before and after each game. And when the game was over, it took a while just to get to the tunnel, because of all the autograph seekers. Sure, I had my ups and downs with injuries of some sort, but that's part of the game. I had nine wonderful seasons playing there. It wasn't until Red Hickey became head coach and installed the shotgun, he felt I was expendable. After my career ended in San Francisco in 1960, I was shuffled off to Minnesota, an expansion team. So was Joe Perry. He went to the Colts and Y.A. was traded to the Giants."

-Hugh McElhenny

Ad featuring Frankie Albert and Kezar Stadium from 1957 LIFE magazine

"Kezar was no ordinary stadium. It was my stadium. I played my high school, college ball, and entire pro career with the 49ers here. I knew every nook and cranny of it. What still gets my goat were those cramped locker rooms. It was built for the basketball players who played at Kezar Pavilion next door. Then we came along, and nothing changed. Imagine about fifty of us crammed in this tiny room at the same time. It was nuts. In fact, we didn't have lockers, we had stalls and no security. Our trainer would collect any valuable from us, like our wallets and keys and give them back after the game. There was only one drinking fountain and three toilets. The benches are still the same height, low to the floor. We took showers in shifts, as there were only four shower heads. Luckily one of the coaches would bring us a few coolers filled with beer while we waited.

One season in the late '50s, we were standing in the dusty East tunnel at Kezar waiting to go onto the field before one game, and the fans already were booing like hell. Tittle, who was going to be introduced first said, 'Please, you go first'. I was the team captain, so I agreed. When I ran out, I forgot there was this little border, a wooden lip about five-inches high, on the track. I tripped on it, and went sprawling. The people were laughing and clapping. At least they stopped booing.

Bob St. Clair and Y.A Tittle congratulate one another after a win

One time at Kezar in 1954, we were playing the Bears. In those days the goal posts were right on the goal line and padded. We were coming down the field for a touchdown, and were on the 1-yard line. The post was on my left and the guard's right. We had just called a play where our fullback, Joe Perry, was to take a direct hand-off into the line. He took the hand-off, ran smack dab into the goal post with his head, veered a little to the right and went across the goal line and scored. I helped him get up and back to the huddle. He was dizzy, and his eyes were going back and forth. Just before we lined up for the conversion, he said, 'Bob, that was a mighty fine hole you opened up for me, but tell me one thing, which one of you bastards missed the linebacker?'

The following season, we were in the middle of a game against the Bears, and I led McElhenny around the end and threw a block. He finally got tackled right in front of the Bears bench. Just before the half, he was trying to get up real fast because time was running out. Guys on top of him were holding him down. So, he kicked the guy to get the hell off of him. As Mac ran back to the huddle, someone in an overcoat, hat and glasses kicked him right in the ass. This guy turned around just as I was going by him. I whacked him on the side of the neck with an elbow, knocking his hat and glasses off, and down he went. As I stopped and turned around, all the Bears ran off the bench and jumped on top of me. It was a hell of a mess. I found out later I had whacked George Halas.

The interesting think about it in those days, nobody got penalized for that stuff. But right after the season was over, Halas called up Tony Morabito, and said he wanted to trade for me. Halas told him any guy who has the spirit and is a good athlete, I want him!

In 2001, the Kezar playing field was named after me -'Bob St. Clair Field'. My first response was 'unbelievable!' If you were born and raised in San Francisco, fortunate to have talent to make it to the Hall of Fame, then find out that they named a field after you where you played – how fortunate can a person be? It's mind boggling. I'm still overwhelmed. Talk about being blessed as an athlete. To think I played my high school ball for Poly, my college games at USF, and the 49ers games on this field - comes full circle. I can still hear the crowd. I loved playing here."

-Bob St. Clair

"My most heartfelt moment at Kezar was after the Bears game in '57. It was the game where our beloved owner Tony Morabito suffered a fatal heart attack. I remember before the game, Tony was in great spirits pumping us all up, and telling us the Bears could be beaten. I recalled the last player Tony talked to before leaving the dressing room was our defensive end, Charley Powell. He told Powell not to let those Bears make him so angry, that he'd do something he'd regret. All the players wept when we heard he died. Albert cried out that he'd have rather lost the game by 100 points than lose Tony. Tony was loved by all us guys."

   -Billy Wilson

"Right around Kezar were a bunch of bars. One I remember was the Kezar Club. The fans would be juiced by the time the game ended, and it could get a little rowdy if things didn't go well. Our quarterback, John Brodie was a frequent target of those fusillades. He reportedly once told Johnny Unitas before a game, 'John if you're going to walk with me, you'd better put on your helmet.' I think of Papa Halas and the Bears and Green Bay ... they played old-style 'smash mouth' football. Kezar was throwback football in a neighborhood, between Golden Gate Park and a bunch of houses. It had a real home feeling to it. Nothing like the big huge stadiums with the big huge parking lots that came after."

   -Gene Washington

"It was at Kezar that the 49er spirit really began. We had a great following. Those were the real '49er Faithful'. The spirit you see today didn't just get started. It's been around for a while. Around 1970-71, our fans may have gotten a little spoiled by the success of our team. Those years we were one of the best teams in the league. Many good people would be surprised if we didn't win. There's nothing deeply I can say about Kezar. The most important thing is that I survived."

   -John Brodie

"I remember the over-enthusiastic fans breaking my car's antenna in the easily-accessible players' parking lot. I also remember a quieter side to Kezar. My fondest memory was Sunday mornings before games. I'd get up early and drive through Golden Gate Park before the park came alive, and it was just so serene. It was so quiet. It was just at peace. And that struck me more than anything."

-Cedric Hardman

"I do remember the whole tone and excitement playing a game at Kezar. I always loved playing there with the mud and the seagulls and the intimate setting. We had a real home field advantage. Often those passionate fans at Kezar booed me after I'd drop a couple of balls, but they inspired me to dish out more punishment to unsuspecting defenders in blocking schemes. Then after games, we'd share a few beers at the Kezar Club, but I always controlled the amount of partying before I drove back home to Alameda. Those were the best of times."

-Monty Stickles

"Kezar Stadium was a wonderful place to play, a stadium many teams were happy to see. All the NFL players liked Kezar. The weather was always good for football. It was cool, unlike New York or Chicago, where it could be very humid or very cold. Kezar was definitely my favorite place to play. The fans were pretty good out there. They could make it hard on some people - quarterbacks especially - but overall they were pretty knowledgeable. They knew their football."

-Bob Toneff

"Kezar had in some very avid football fans, where they were able to show what they thought. I witnessed a lot of exchanges between the fans and players, some good and some very disturbing."

-Ed Beard

"I remember going to Kezar on game days. After breakfast at the team hotel, Matt Hazeltine and I would drive over to Kezar around 10:00 a.m. for home games. We'd drive down Haight Street on Sunday mornings, because that was the entrance to Golden Gate Park. It was when the hippies were coming around. Sunday was the big day for them outside Kezar. It was interesting. I'll put it at that. That's kind of a funny thing to remember, but it's what I remember most about the place."

-Ken Willard

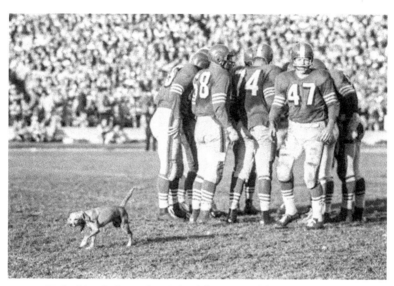

Dicky Moegle (no. 47) and the defense unveil their secret weapon

Kezar was my domain. Of all the NFL stadiums I played, Kezar was the best. They had the most passionate fans in the league, and always treated me like family. Maybe it's because I was like the Deion Sanders in my day, playing anywhere they needed me - offense, defense and special teams. I was a safety man for kickoffs, and sometime for punts. I played defensive back, and with McElhenny down with a foot injury during the 1955 season, I played halfback as well. When I think about playing at Kezar, they were the best years of my football career."

-Dicky Moegle

Len Eshmont Award Winers 1957-1970

Given each year to the 49ers player who best exemplifies the "inspirational and courageous play" of Len Eshmont, a player from the original 1946 49ers team.

1957	QB	**Y. A. Tittle**	1964	DT	**Charlie Krueger**
1958	FB	**Joe Perry**	1965	QB	**John Brodie**
1959	HB	**J.D. Smith**	1966	HB	**John David Crow**
1960	S	**Dave Baker**	1967	HB	**John David Crow**
1961	DT	**Leo Nomellini**	1968	LB	**Matt Hazeltine**
1962	DE	**Dan Colchico**	1969	CB	**Jimmy Johnson**
1963	T	**Bob St. Clair**	1970	S	**Roosevelt Taylor**

"My mother carried me in her womb into Kezar. We had a long involvement with the team. Dad did the TV play-by-play, while I was a ball boy. Back then there was a family section in the press box, and we had two seats. I sat there often with my mom. Hugh McElhenny is still her favorite player. We got to know so many of the 49ers. It wasn't all that unusual to have them over for dinner - Tittle, St. Clair, Nomellini. The players with the 49ers it seemed stayed together forever."

-Dan Fouts

"The place was a dump – pigeons pooped on you, swirling winds killed the passing game and there were only two shower heads in the visitor's locker room."

-Art Donovan

"In 1949, I was playing offensive end for Fort Ord's football team. On weekends we would go to see the 49ers play at 'Kazoo' (Kezar) where I fell in love with football. Sittin' there I saw a player from the Yankees miss a whole mess of tackles. So when I got back to the Fort, I jotted down a letter to Coach Shaw. All I done was tell Shaw that I had a good pair of hands, and why not? Nothing' lost, nothing' gained. Well, Shaw – who is called the 'Grey Fox' - he jotted me back a letter, but I never did activate on it."

-Dick "Night Train" Layne

"A cracked skull, a couple of broken fingers, some missing teeth, a dislocated ankle and a bloody nose was what I remember from playing at Kezar. The 49ers showed they knew very little of rules governing those different points. They took special delight in butting heads with us, and the player who could spill the most blood was considered one of their best players. I'm referring to Hardy Brown."

-Troy Ledbetter

8

Reflections

"Watching games at Kezar were the best ever. That old saying, 'the team that stays together, plays together and wins together'. That's the way it was in the 1950's and '60s. John Brodie, Bob St. Clair and Leo Nomellini played their whole careers with the team.

After the 49ers left Kezar for Candlestick, friend Vince and I decided to visit Kezar one last time in 1983. The stadium was still being used for local high school games. On a bright sunny Thursday afternoon, we decided to take the afternoon off to watch a Lincoln-Mission game, maybe see some old friends, who would surely be there, take in a good game and naturally, eat our hot dogs. Vince played here in the '60s for Lincoln High, and he remembered crowds of 10,000 on Turkey

Day. He said the hot dogs always tasted better at Kezar. We talked about our high school days, the old prep pageants that opened the season for screaming rooters, almost 50,000 of them, along with the cheerleaders, bands and drill teams. Those were unforgettable spectacles.

We were late for the kickoff. The parking lot was empty. Ticket booths were boarded shut. We thought maybe the game had been scheduled for another field, but noticed an open gate at the East entrance. The gate man charged $2, and we thought that wasn't bad – about the same admission as 49ers games when they started in the late '40s.

Once inside, we were amazed to see the playing field in such beautiful condition. We were more amazed that, besides the players and cheerleaders, we counted 15 spectators for Lincoln and 12 for Mission. It was a shock to us, because it seemed like yesterday there were

59,000 cheering 49ers fans packed into Kezar for a pro game. We also noticed the scoreboards were not working, and the clock wasn't moving. We decided to walk around trying to learn the score, and get our hot dogs. But all concession stands were boarded shut. We found a janitor who said, 'Are you men scouts, 'cause there ain't no folks in the stands?'

As we strolled around, now oblivious to the contest and the noise on the field below, we found graffiti on the walls referring to the 49ers of the '60s. In an open storage room were rows of dusty folding chairs once needed for the press box, which sheltered the 49ers owner and their friends. The rest was imagination. Down at the end zone was where R.C. Owens caught his first alley-oop pass from Y.A. Tittle to beat the LA Rams. Over near that bench was the spot where an irate 49er fan ran onto the field to take a swing at Chicago coach George Halas, and instead was kicked in the pants by Halas's son. It was time to leave Kezar, and for the last time. It was one of the saddest days of our lives."

-Art Rosenbaum

"Kezar doesn't look exactly as it did back in the day. The original stadium suffered a great deal of damage in the earthquake devastating much of the Bay Area. As a result, it was torn down and reconstructed into a 10,000-seat venue, but is a great tribute to the history of the area and all of the great moments that occurred there. I would love to say the same thing about the Polo Grounds, Cleveland Stadium or even Three Rivers Stadium, but no remnants remain from these historic stadiums."

-George Maderos

"There was no reprieve for Kezar in 1989. Its bleachers were chopped up and sold in pieces, while 1,500 people partied and said so long to the city's once 'Grand Canyon of Football'. The 'Good-bye to Old Kezar' bash was inside a huge tent in the middle of the football field. It was a lovely affair. They charged $30 a head to shake hands with old legends, and revisit old memories. Dilapidated Kezar, the birthplace of the 49ers and dizzying football folklore, was demolished after that, sprouting a new smaller and fancier facility for high school football."

-Clarence Johnson

"I have many memories of Kezar. In April '89, the Niners held a good-bye to Kezar night just prior to the stadium being demolished. A huge tent was thrown over the field at one end with orchestra and many former players appeared at the event. Talk about mixed emotions: on one hand I had to cover the story for the *Contra Costa Times*. On the other hand, I wanted to talk to the greats just as a fan. The thrill of the night for me was standing with Joe Montana on the 50-yard line. Monty Stickles, tight end, told me he was bitter about the stadium being torn down. He said he could look down into the stadium from his apartment window, and it made him upset every time he did. 'They're going to destroy Kezar? Makes no sense'. Joe 'the Jet' Perry, running back, said, 'In '49, I took a pitch-out right here against the Chicago Rockets, and ran around end for a touchdown. No one knew a fullback could run that fast.' Other memories: 'With seconds left in a 1962 game against the Lions, Detroit lined up for a field goal to tie the score. As the ball was snapped, Hall of Famer Leo Nomellini hoisted safety Dave Baker on his shoulders to reach high to try and block the kick. Wayne Walker's kick sailed through to tie the score. End of game. No sudden death in those days'."

-Dennis Caracciolo

"I was a 49ers season ticket holder the entire time the team played at Kezar. The stadium today is quite lovely. Gone are the tall concrete walls that once housed 59,000 fans. You can still stroll along the track inside among the green lawns with no worry about flying beer bottles and cans. I noticed between the yard lines on the North side of the field, there were seats, not benches. When I used to attend games there, I remember our seats were cramped, offering about 16-inches of space for a patron's posterior. And those puny locker rooms the team used wouldn't be big enough today to fit a single star's entourage."

-Cory Nelson

Kezar Stadium and Bob St. Clair Field 2020

"When the Niners and Kezar became fruition, my life changed forever. I have 24-years of wonderful memories of Kezar. It was our home of fanaticism for my wife and me. The new and smaller stadium I call 'Little Kezar,' but it still possesses the spirit of what was once built for us crazed Niner fans. The triumphal archway to the west says Kezar Stadium is very similar to the early scheme of the original stadium. On my 82nd birthday, I met with the Neptune Society to arrange my cremation. My ashes will be scattered at Kezar with all the 49er greats!"

-R. Pondexter

9

Memorable Games

October 9, 1949 **49ers 56**, **Browns 28**

Before a Kezar Stadium throng of 59,770, the 49ers beat their
perennial tormentors, the Cleveland Browns 56-28. The 49ers
management estimated it had to return orders for another 40,000 tickets,
so eager were the fans to see the 49ers, who by beating the Browns,
could take over first place in the standings. The 49ers hadn't beaten
Cleveland since their first meeting in 1946, but who had? In their four
seasons, the Browns had lost only three games, and were unbeaten in
their last 29 starts. Adding to the game's appeal to fans was the Browns
last appearance at Kezar in the next-to-last game of 1948.

In 1948, the Browns were en route to a 14-0 record - 15-0, if you count their 49-7 championship game victory over the Buffalo Bills. In beating the 49ers earlier in the season, they had held the 49ers to seven points, a tribute to the Browns defense. The 49ers weren't accustomed to scoring so little. The week before, the 49ers had scored 44 points against the Chicago Rockets; the week after, they scored 63 against the Brooklyn Dodgers. In fact, coming into the 1948 game at Kezar, the 49ers had lost only the game in Cleveland. In the rematch, the 49ers were a six-point favorite.

As the game unfolded the 49ers fell behind 10-0, then scored two second period touchdowns to lead the Browns 14-10 at halftime. The most memorable play that half was a 29-yard run by John Strzykalski. In those days, you could get up after being knocked down. So he did. He spent more time on the ground than on his feet. But in the second half, the Browns outscored the 49ers three touchdowns to two, and won the game 31-28.

On the afternoon of October 9, 1949, the Browns once again visited Kezar. This time the odds favored Cleveland. By the fourth quarter, a patriarch who was sitting in the press box, had turned to those surrounding him and said, 'For this one day, this is the greatest football team I have ever seen'.

He meant the 49ers. In this game Frankie Albert produced five touchdowns, all by passing. Joe Perry, Strzykalski and Paul Carr each scored twice, and Alyn Beals, Nick Susoeff - once each. Defensive end,

Frankie Albert avoids Browns pass rush

Hal Shoener, twice escaped blockers and hit Otto Graham causing two fumbles resulting in turnovers. Graham didn't do all that badly, as he threw three touchdowns. Perry got 156 yards on 11 carries, while the Browns great Marion Motley got 89 yards on 13 carries. Albert completed 16 of 24 passes for 242 yards. In addition to his five passing touchdowns, he had another that went 42 yards to the 1-yard line, leading to a touchdown on the following play.

As Prescott Sullivan wrote in the *Examiner*, "It was indeed the pent-up fury of three-years of frustration. But fury begets fury, as in that 1949 game, which was one of the most physical games ever between these two rivals".

October 4, 1953 **49ers 31, Rams 30**

Up into 1970, the 49ers record against the Los Angeles Rams was 10-10-1 at Kezar. In 1953, the Rams came to Kezar as favorites. Many 49ers fans were convinced this game was one of the greatest of all, between these two teams. The 49ers believe they won it, though coach Buck Shaw wasn't quite sure how, while Rams coach Hampton Pool wasn't convinced his team lost. On this day, Hugh McElhenny made runs of 93 and 71 yards, but the 93-yarder was called back because of a penalty. It was on a punt return for an apparent touchdown, but Bob St. Clair was caught clipping Rams end, Andy Robustelli. When McElhenny broke loose on the 71-yard run in the final moments of the game to set up one of the wildest finishes in memory at Kezar, that play might have zapped "The King". Rams defensive back, Woodley Lewis, caught him on the 9-yard line. McElhenny later admitted had he been fresh, Lewis would never had touched him.

Joe Perry sweeps wide against a Rams defender

Coach Pool of the Rams had warned his players in advance that they could not let up on McElhenny. His advice was on par with telling a baseball team to watch out for a Bob Feller fastball. Coach Shaw also had some pregame advice for his players. It consisted of extra practice sessions to sharpen the 49ers defense against the Rams passing attack. It paid off, as Rams quarterback, Norm Van Brocklin, was limited to 20 completions of 34 passes and a mere 272 yards in all.

The 49ers fell behind early, 20-0, as the fans were becoming restless. Sporadically, beer cans and cushions sailed onto the playing field from the stands. The game turned around in the second quarter, as a fourth down pass to Dick "Night Train" Lane was dropped. The 49ers took over with a first down at the Rams 28-yard line. In five plays, Y.A. Tittle moved the 49ers to a touchdown with a short pass to Billy Wilson. At halftime it was Rams 20, 49ers 7. After that, the momentum swung with the 49ers. They took the second half kickoff and moved 68 yards to another touchdown in 14 plays, (all but two of them passes) making it 20-14. The scoring play was delicately deliberate. It began with a Tittle-to-McElhenny pitch-out. Seven Rams leaped on McElhenny, but he lateraled the ball to Joe Perry, who carried it into the end zone.

The Rams countered, as they drove 90 yards in 11 plays. Tank Younger scored a touchdown, increasing the Rams lead to 27-14. A few plays later, 49ers defensive back, Lowell Wagner, fell on a Van Brocklin fumble, and the opportunistic 49ers turned it into a touchdown on a Joe Perry 11-yard run, making the score 27-21. In a reversal of fortune, it came to the 49ers in the final period. Rex Berry intercepted a Norm Van Brocklin pass at the Rams 48-yard line and returned it to the 30. In seven plays the 49ers scored again, as rookie halfback Billy Mixon did the honors with a 4-yard burst. Soltau kicked the extra point and the 49ers were in front, 28-27.

Then the Rams took the ball and moved down field to the 49ers 11-yard line with a fourth down and inches to go. Rams coach Pool had a good set of alternatives, as you can have when you trail by a point. He sent in Ben Agajanian for a field goad attempt. He made the field goal and it pushed the Rams out front 30-28. With under three minutes remaining in the game, Tittle broke the huddle, and he made a glorious decision. He audibled at the line of scrimmage. He knew the Rams defense would play deep. Instead, Tittle threw a screen pass to McElhenny. One Ram had a shot at the "King" and in the bewilderment of the moment, failed to bring him down. Tremendous blocks by the 49ers Leo Nomellini, Bruno Banducci, and Billy Wilson, sprung McElhenny into

179

the open down the sidelines, all the way to the Rams 9-yard line. The play covered 71 yards. With the clock winding down, the 49ers moved the ball to the Ram 5-yard line. In Tittle's zeal, he had failed to get the ball in front of the goal posts for Soltau's winning kick. By now, the clock showed 42 seconds to play, and still moving. Tittle kept the 49ers in the huddle for the full 30 seconds. And in doing so, the 49ers got penalized 5 yards back to the 10, but reduced the angle for Soltau. This strategy came as a revelation to coach Shaw. He later confessed he almost had a heart attack after he sent in Soltau to try the field goal. Y.A. took so much time off the clock, he thought he would never get the kick away before the final gun. Soltau kicked the ball through the uprights and the referee's arms shot up, and the 49ers beat the Rams 31-30. Tittle commented after the game that he was completely confident - not only getting off the field goal attempt, but that it would be good.

October 27, 1957 **49ers 21, Bears 17**

The afternoon was cold and gloomy in San Francisco. Fog had billowed in early from the Pacific, three miles to the west of Kezar, and hung like a pall over the capacity crowd of nearly 60,000. It wasn't the weather, however, that depressed the spirits of those crammed into the ancient bowl. They had watched in disbelief and despair, as their beloved 49ers dropped two scores behind the Bears. They fumbled the opening kickoff, which led to a Bears touchdown. Soon after, a 51-yard touchdown pass from Ed Brown to Harlon Hill made it 14-0. Tony Morabito, the proud owner of the 49ers, said he could not blame the fans for being angry and disappointed. He went on to say the 49ers had the best fans in the country, and the team has let them down so many times. He also had a hunch this ball club wouldn't fold.

After a pep talk by Y.A. Tittle to his teammates, the 49ers showed some aggression. They began to act as if they had heard the voice of confidence by their employer. Joe Arenas returned a punt 18 yards; line plunges by Gene Babb, interspersed with passes to Billy Wilson and Clyde Conner, took the ball to the Bear one, and Y.A. sneaked it across for a touchdown. The stadium rocked with the traditional 49ers chant of "Go! Go! Go!" The Bears George Blanda kicked a 26-yard field goal just as the half ended. The 49ers trailed the Bears 17-7.

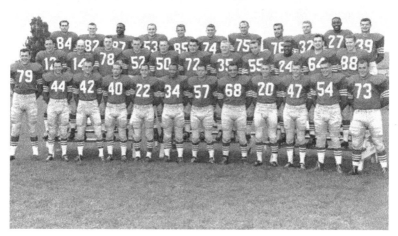

1957 San Francisco 49ers

The second half started with the Bears getting the ball. On the third play of the third quarter, Brown tried a roll-out and was thrown for a five-yard loss by 49ers defensive tackle, Bill Herchman. At that point tragedy struck. Tony Morabito, sitting in the press box had suffered a heart attack. Dr. Frank Cox, sitting nearby, immediately began applying artificial respiration while Tony's brother, Vic, raced down the steps and across the field to summon Dr. Bill O'Grady, the team's and Tony's physician. Father William McGuire gave Final Absolution to Morabito, who was then rushed to St. Mary's Hospital. Midway through the third period, Dr. O'Grady brought dreaded news from the hospital to the 49ers bench that Morabito had passed away. There was a moment of stunned silence, then the bench became a madhouse of crying, shouting players. From that moment on, the 49ers caught fire. Defensive end, Charley Powell, charged in and threw Will Gilmore for an 11-yard loss. On the next play, defensive tackle, Leo Nomellini, with tears streaming down his face, savagely rushed in at Brown, who was attempting to pass. The ball was picked off by Bill Herchman on the 49ers 46-yard line, and convoyed by Bob Toneff, took it 54-yards for a 49ers touchdown, cutting the Bears lead to 17-14.

As the fourth quarter began, once again a Brown pass was deflected by linebacker Marv Matuszak, and intercepted by cornerback Dicky Moegle, who dodged and twisted his way for 40-yards all the way down to the Bears 19-yard line. Joe Perry, despite a knee injury, boomed ahead for another 8 yards to the 11-yard line. Tittle then found Wilson in the right flat, who took it in for the touchdown, and the 49ers forged ahead 21-17. After the ensuing kick-off, 49ers safety J.D. Smith intercepted another Brown pass. And just before the final gun, the Bears had reached the 49ers 13, as quarterback Zeke Bratkowski, subbing for a battered Brown, threw a pass intended for Hill in the end zone, but Moegle, playing his greatest game as a 49er, made his third interception of the day, and returned it 29 yards.

Defensive end, Ed Henke who had given every ounce of his energy, collapsed from sheer exhaustion, as Tittle held the ball on the final play of the game, then dropped to his knees. It was a bittersweet victory, but Morabito was right - the 49ers didn't fold.

November 3, 1957 **49ers 35, Lions 31**

The 1957 season was a season in which the 49ers and Lions would tie for a division title - the furthest the 49ers had ever advanced in NFL league play. And, the game that made a playoff possible was this November encounter at Kezar. Just before the game started, Norm Standlee, an original 49er from the 1946 team, got on the stadium loudspeaker and asked for a minute of standing prayer to the memory of Tony Morabito, who had suffered his fatal heart attack during the previous Sunday's

49ers come-from-behind win over the Bears at Kezar. And today, once again the 49ers found a way to win the hard way, as the whirling, vertical, "alley-oop" of the flanker back, R.C. Owens won another football game for the 49ers, 35-31.

Owens, a specialist in mushrooming straight-up from the ground, and returning with the football in his grasp, caught a Y.A. Tittle pass that sailed from the 41-yard line to the end zone. The unbelievable catch was made with exactly 11 seconds remaining on the clock. It turned certain defeat into spectacular victory over the Lions. It was unbelievable, except that this had become the typical "alley-oop" of Owens, who was crossing the 15-yard line when the ball was thrown, and who was ten feet in the air at the East end zone when the ball arrived. Defending him were two of the most experienced pass defenders in the NFL, Jack Christensen and Jim David. The two white-shirted Lions and one red-shirt 49er leaped together, but only Owens, a magnificence in rhythm, was able to pluck the flying ball for the third time in the regular season (once each against the Rams and Bears at Kezar). A full house of Kezar fandom – 59,702 – roared and stomped, and then asked each other: "How? Tell me how did he do it?"   .

Only two minutes and nine seconds earlier, the Lions had snatched victory from what seemed certain defeat, when a Hugh McElhenny fumble was recovered by the Lions on the 49ers seven yard line. On second down a pass to the left corner from Tobin Rote to Jim Doran, plus Bobby Layne's conversion, put the Lions in front 31-28. Previously, the 49ers had bounced back from an 0-10 second quarter deficit to a 14-10 lead at the half, and a 28-10 lead into the fourth quarter. Then the Lions fought back, aided by 49ers miscues, enabling them to take the lead with 1:20 left to play. With the 49ers facing a crushing defeat, the Tittle to R.C. "alley-oop" Owens closed the show.

December 8, 1957 **49ers 17, Colts 13**

Comng into the 11th week of the season, the 49ers were tied with Baltimore and Detroit for first place in the Western Conference with identical 6-4 records, and just two games remaining. 49ers fans knew the importance of this game. The day before the game, 49ers fans escorted by a police squad on horseback, lined up outside Kezar to buy the remaining 5,000 tickets that went on sale in the morning. The long lines rolled back into Golden Gate Park, while some 15,000 fans unable to get seats for the game poured out of the city, and headed anywhere beyond the boundaries of the 150+ mile TV blackout.

Gordy Soltau boots a field goal against the Colts

The game with the Colts lived up to the billing. Almost immediately on the 49ers opening drive, the Colts were called for pass interference on Hugh McElhenny on the one-yard line, and the 49ers scored first. The Colts quickly tied it up, as Milt Davis picked off a Y.A. Tittle pass and ran 75 yards for a score to trail 7-6. Leo Nomellini blocked the conversion. In the second quarter, Gordy Soltau booted the 49ers further ahead, 10-6. Still, throughout the afternoon the Colts often appeared to have the sounder team. Johnny Unitas, the Colts remarkable quarterback, handled his team well, although he was under strong pressure from the 49ers defensive line of Ed Henke, Bob Toneff, Matt Hazeltine, Marv Matuszak, Bill Herchman and Kari Rubke most of the afternoon.

Unitas worked carefully to set up the most spectacular touchdown of the game, an 82-yard scoring pass to halfback Lenny Moore. This put Baltimore in front 13-10, with four minutes and 36 seconds into the third quarter. Halfback McElhenny, filling in for end Clyde Conner, aided the 49ers of much needed speed at the end and flanker position. He had already caught seven passes for 153 yards that afternoon.

The score see-sawed back and forth, as both defenses dominated the game until late in the fourth quarter. With just under a minute left to play in the game, Tittle maneuvered the 49ers down into scoring position with a 43-yard pass play to McElhenny. But Tittle, who was 21 for 34 tosses, injured his hand on the play when the Colts defense converged on him causing a sudden muscle spasm in his injured leg. Two teammates assisted him off the field.

Coach Frankie Albert had no choice but to send inexperienced rookie quarterback, John Brodie, onto the field. Brodie, who had played something less than 10-minutes through the 10 previous games had the Western Conference title riding in his hands. He tried one pass from the 14-yard line, which went astray. With 0:47 seconds left on the clock, knowing a tie was useless to them in their quest for their first division championship, the 49ers huddled facing fourth down. With the 49ers trailing by only 3 points, it seemed logical to fans that the sure-footed Soltau could have tied the game.

The rookie signal caller asked his teammates, "What the hell do we do now?" McElhenny spoke up. "Davis is playing me too loose. Just throw it to the left corner of the end zone and I'll be there". Under a heavy pass rush, McElhenny raced straight down at defensive back, Milt Davis, and suddenly cut sharply to the sideline. The pass was thrown perfectly. McElhenny gathered it in for the winning score. "I just threw it and prayed," Brodie said. Team captain Bob St. Clair awarded the game ball to McElhenny. "Usually we like to give the ball to a defensive player", St. Clair said in his presentation speech. "But today, Mac's the man".

GAMEDAY PROGRAMS

Memories of being a 49ers fan at Kezar may be triggered by a glimpse into a game day program. 49ers programs created a public image of San Francisco and the team. The cover art showing diversified themes, fostered traditions and emotions surrounding the game experience. Programs provide windows to the past, and are significant and collectible pieces of popular culture. During the 49ers founding years, they hired Lederer, Street & Zeus Company in Berkeley to print their programs. The 32-page program sold for a quarter. They contained skillfully written articles, photos and biographies, stats, line-ups and advertisements. The original cover artwork was illustrated by William Kay that depicted humorous cartoon illustrations of a 49ers gold miner, clad in boots and a lumberjack shirt, firing a pair of pistols, while tormenting the opposition. Program cover artists include:

1946-48 **William Kay**

1949-51 **Louis Macouillard, Vic Couillard**

1952-61 **R. Vrooman, H. Swanberg, Harry Bonath, Larry Tisdale, C.C. Beall, Lon Keller, John Murphy, Howard Brodie**

1962-67 **Joe Little, Tran Mawicke, Lon Feck, Courtney Mouth, Gary Thomas, Martyn Hett**

1968-70 program covers used photographic images

Program cover from the first 49ers game at Kezar

December 22, 1957 **Lions 31, 49ers 27**

The 1957 NFL Western Division playoff was such a milestone for the San Francisco 49ers. After winning the last three games against New York, Baltimore and Green Bay, the 49ers were 8-4, and tied with

Detroit atop the NFL's Western Division standings. The 49ers were 1-1 in two games with the Lions edging them at home 35-31, then losing in Detroit 31-10.

Kezar Stadium was filled with 60,180 fans waiting for the curtain to go up on the 49ers Black Sunday. The Lions and the 49ers squared off at 1:00 p.m. on December 22, 1957. The first half was a 49ers blow-out. Y.A. Tittle was 12 for 19 passing, including a first quarter 34-yard alley-oop touchdown pass to R.C. Owens, and scoring tosses to Hugh McElhenny and Billy Wilson. Gordy Soltau's field goad made it a 24-7 laugher. When the halftime gun went off, the 49ers took the locker room with visions of their first NFL championship since joining the league in 1950.

49ers championship game phantom ticket

How overconfident the 49ers were at halftime remains arguable. What is certain is that after the 49ers mastered a 24-7 lead, the Kezar printing presses had already turned out 49ers versus Cleveland Browns NFL championship tickets. Falstaff beer flowed like buttermilk, and the San Francisco football world did everything, except plan a jubilant Market Street parade.

The public address announcer was announcing that anybody interested in obtaining championship tickets, they would be on sale the following week. "I told the guys," said Joe Schmidt, Lions linebacker, "they are already selling championship tickets…that's exactly how they (the 49ers) feel about you (the Lions). Let's go out and play a tough second half, and see what can happen".

When the second half clock started ticking, the Lions house was already on fire. A metamorphosis was about to transform Kezar dominions. The 49ers domination turned into slow water torture for the fans. The last 30-minutes became heartbreaking 49ers football.

The third quarter began well enough for the 49ers. With 2:22 elapsed, McElhenny took a Tittle screen pass, and reeled off a thrilling 71-yard run. But, a Lions wall rose up from the Kezar turf, and stopped the 49ers cold at the 19. Led by Joe Schmidt, the Lions defense roared back, blitzed Tittle mercilessly and reduced the "Million-Dollar Backfield" to spare change. A Soltau field goal made it 27-7, but the 49ers scoring machine was dismantled. It was an era in which quarterbacks called their own plays, and Tittle readily acknowledges a switch to conservative play-calling in the second half. "I played a guarded game", he said. "I didn't throw in the second half and I remember looking at the clock. It would be third and six and I'd call a draw".

After McElhenny's run, the bottom simply fell out for the 49ers. Although he hadn't carried the ball in his last four games, Detroit's Tom "The Bomb" Tracy (filling in for banged-up John Henry Johnson) scored on runs of one and 58 yards. The 49ers lead was sliced to 27-21. Legendary quarterback Bobby Layne (who had broken his leg weeks before) watched on crutches as his stand-in, Tobin Rote, performed like a yeoman. When the 49ers began to key on Tracy, Rote hit receiver Steve Junker (8 receptions, 92 yards). The San Francisco back-breaker occurred 44 seconds into the fourth quarter, when Gene Gedman scored on a two-yard plunge.

The unthinkable had happened. Detroit took the lead 28-27 on Jim Martin's point-after kick. Had a pin dropped under the old Flying A scoreboard clock in Kezar at that moment, the sound would have been heard on Van Ness Avenue. As Lions coach George Wilson said, "Never were so many touchdowns scored in dead silence". The fourth quarter saw the 49ers turn the ball over four times, including three Tittle interceptions and a Perry fumble (Perry broke his jaw in the game). With time running out, the 49ers faithful had to be envisioning the most dramatic San Francisco sports finish ever. 49ers salvation was destined to arrive in a Tittle-to-Owens "alley-oop" in the final seconds. Tittle himself was thinking the same thing. "We hoped to get close enough for an 'alley-ooper' to R.C.", Tittle said 50-years later. "I was trying that, when a guy hit my hand, and Roger Zatkoff intercepted." It was Tittle's last throw of the season. A paralyzed 49er world watched in disbelief, as Martin's 13-yard field goal clinched it for Detroit. The Lions had scored three touchdowns in 4:29. All hope drained from the hearts of 49ers fans, and the curtain came down on their championship dreams: Lions 31, 49ers 27. The 49ers had blown a 20-point lead.

Y.A. Tittle and teammates downcast in defeat

Game over, Lions players enter Kezar locker room

In the post-game locker room, owner Vic Morabito sat alone, then quietly spoke to players individually. An emotional Billy Wilson, who caught nine passes for 107 yards collapsed with his head in his hands. Perry, his jaw broken, was unable to speak, and used sign language to communicate with reporters. A grim Frankie Albert told reporters, "We won the first half and they won the second. Of course, it was mistakes, fumbles and interceptions which beat us. Tittle's pass protection broke down in the second half."

Says losing quarterback Y.A. Tittle, "I've blanked that loss out of my mind forever. I wiped it off the memory chart."

Fifty years later, it can be said that what the Lions heard in the locker room, was in all likelihood Albert's spirited halftime cheer. But, the Lions misread it as chutzpah, and it became the psychological edge they needed to shut down the 49ers explosive offense, while rolling-up 24 unanswered points. Thus, one of the most memorable playoff comebacks in NFL history can be attributed to bad stadium acoustics. With or without the locker room fiasco, the comeback could not have been accomplished without the legends in the Lions lineup.

Six Lions on the field that day made it into the NFL Hall of Fame, although Layne and Johnson were not in uniform. The others included Schmidt, who later became the Lions coach; safeties Jack Christiansen and Yale Lary; and tackle Lou Creekmur. George Wilson, the Detroit coach, said the turning point was when McElhenny was stopped inside the 10, denying the 49ers the end zone early in the third quarter. "So McElhenny runs 71 yards," he said, "but we hold and force the 49ers to kick a field goal from the three. That turned it."

49ers tackle, Bob St. Clair, had a different version of the loss. He said, "After the Lions put-in quarterback Tobin Rote in the third quarter, all three of our defensive backs went down. Poor Albert, our coach, was looking up and down the row to see whom we could put in. We had offensive backs, but they didn't know how to play defense - so Rote had a field day, and took advantage of the situation. They killed us. We get down to the four or five-yard line early in the third quarter, and Perry took a direct hand-off over me on the line and scored. But, the referee said I was offside. If we had scored that touchdown, it would have been enough that Detroit could not have made it back. Instead of upping our lead to 31-7, we settled for a 27-7 lead. The following day we watched game film and it showed I wasn't offside. I was just ahead of everyone else. If the referee had seen what really happened, I'm sure we would have won. As for many players on that '57 team, it still hurts to talk about it to this day".

The following morning San Francisco newspaper headlines read: "SAN FRANCISCO HAS IT, DROPS IT"…"IN LIKE LAMBS, OUT LIKE LIONS". The Detroit Free Press ran the banner: "THE LIONS' 1957 FIGHT SONG: WE WON BECAUSE WE WON!"

--Dennis Caracciolo

(Published in the *San Jose Mercury News* 12-22-2007)

December 10, 1961 **49ers 22**, **Packers 21**

"Great!"

That one word by Coach Red Hickey summed up the job quarterback John Brodie did at Kezar, when he engineered the 49ers to a tingling 22-21 victory over the Western Division champion Green Bay Packers, and ultimate 1961 World Champions. The game turned out to be one of Brodie's most memorable games of his career.

Captain Matt Hazeltine pointed out it was Brodie who called the daring fourth down gamble early in the fourth quarter, in which he ran from field goal formation, making it three yards and a first down by inches. That play enabled Brodie to move the ball downfield closer into field goal range, where tommy Davis kicked a 10-yard field goal, increasing the 49ers lead to 19-14. Brodie said he called the play because he didn't think Davis's chances of kicking a field goal from 47 yards out against the wind would make it. "That took a lot of guts", said Hazeltine.

Brodie completed 19 of 29 for 328 yards and two touchdowns, and 13 first downs passing against the number one defense in the NFL. Against huge odds the game was a tribute to Tommy Davis, R.C. Owens

(7 catches for 127 yards), Bernie Casey (5 catches for 118 yards), Abe Woodson (47 kick-off return) and Jimmy Johnson's 63-yard interception of a Bart Starr pass, which set up the 49ers first score, and a dozen others who made steel-cable out of thread, and reeled in a winner against seemingly insurmountable odds.

Late in the fourth quarter with the 49ers holding a 19-14 lead, Green Bay bounced right back with a 73-yard drive culminated by Jim Taylor's four-yard score. Paul Hornung kicked the extra point to move the Packers ahead 21-19 with 3:12 left to play. "Thar she blows again!" was the reaction of a frustrated 49ers fan.

Bart Starr, Packers quarterback, faces 49ers defense

Hope for the 49ers was renewed in a hurry, as Woodson took Hornung's kickoff, and scampered 46 quick yards before a Packer tripped him up. Then Brodie's magnificent passing was even more accurate than his statistics. One pass to Owens for 15 yards put the 49ers within range of their game winning field goal. "He put that ball right in the bucket, just over the defensive man's head and into my arms. It couldn't have been more perfect", said Owens.

Was Brodie nervous, as he battled the clock on the drive to the winning field goal? "I sure was, until we got down to field goal range," he replied. "But after that, I wasn't. We had two timeouts left. I waited until there were 14 seconds left on the clock and called time out. You can't cut it too close. I saw that there were a host of photographers and reporters behind the goal posts, from where Davis was setting up for the winning kick. At first it looked as if the ball sailed too wide to the right. It was close alright. To say the least, this win didn't come easy".

"Whew!"

January 3, 1971 **Cowboys 17, 49ers 10**

On Sunday, Jan. 3, 1971, 49ers head coach Dick Nolan started that day with a bounce, and an uncharacteristic smile. After he struggled in his first two seasons with the 49ers, things had clicked for Nolan. His team had gone 10-3-1 in the 1970 regular season, and was on a three-game winning streak. The last two wins had been particularly notable.

First, the 49ers went over to Oakland, forced nine turnovers on a wet, sloppy field, and throttled the Raiders 38-7 in the initial regular-season meeting between the Bay Area rivals. Then, the 49ers traveled to frigid Minnesota, and beat the Vikings 17-14 for their first playoff victory. This was a team virtually without a postseason history. The only other time the 49ers had made the postseason resulted in a 31-27 Western Conference playoff loss to the Detroit Lions in 1957. But, Nolan was optimistic that Sunday, heading into an NFC championship game against the Dallas Cowboys in the final professional football game at old Kezar Stadium -- the 49ers home since 1946.

"There was real excitement about the whole thing", Nolan said. "We went in thinking we could win. We knew we had to play an exceptional game, because they had all the experience - especially in pressure games - and this was the first time this had happened to us. But we had really good players, and they'd worked hard to get there".

Head coach Dick Nolan

The 49ers had the NFL's highest-scoring offense, directed by quarterback John Brodie, the league's MVP, and a tough defense led by the likes of future Hall of Famers Dave Wilcox and Jimmy Johnson. And they seemingly had a unique insight into how to attack the Cowboys "flex" defense. Nolan had helped install and run it, as a Dallas assistant in the early 1960s under head coach Tom Landry, an old friend and former defensive backfield teammate with the New York Giants.

As it turned out, however, Nolan's knowledge didn't help much as the Cowboys, struggling to exorcise their own playoff demons, flexed their muscles at cold and windy Kezar. The Landry defense held the 49ers to just 61 yards rushing. The Nolan defense, designed early in the action to retard receivers like the speedy Bob Hayes, couldn't handle the Cowboys rushing game, and rookie running back Duane Thomas, who would gain 143 of his team's 229 yards on the ground. "You stop our run, we throw to Hayes," Cowboys quarterback Craig Morton said. "You stop Hayes, and we run".

With the big rushing disparity, the teams were tied 3-3 at halftime.

"We went in at the half pretty down", Landry said. "The players came in mumbling. They'd played terrible ball the last couple of minutes". But then, early in the third quarter, Dallas got the break that turned the game. From deep in his own territory, Brodie tried to throw the ball away against a Dallas blitz, and Cowboys linebacker Lee Roy Jordan snatched it inches off the ground, and returned it to the 49ers 13-yard line. "I was trying to dump the ball into the ground, but the guy made a hell of play", Brodie said. On first down from the 13, Thomas momentarily misread his blocking, but then swung inside, broke two tackles and scored, as the Cowboys took a 10-3 lead. Dallas went ahead 17-3 before Brodie finally connected with Dick Witcher on a 26-yard touchdown pass over Herb Adderley, to cut the advantage to 17-10.

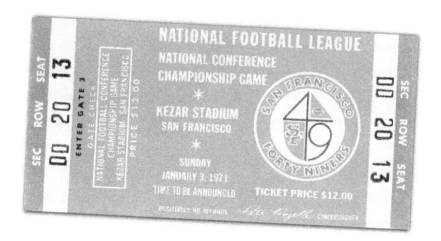

Early in the fourth quarter, Brodie drove his team to the Dallas 44, and then passed accurately to Witcher at the five, but Witcher was unable to hold the ball - one of several crucial near-miss passes for the 49ers that day. Witcher protested that he had been interfered with by Cowboys defensive back Charlie Waters, and replays seemed to confirm that. But no penalty was called, and there was no more scoring. The 49ers had played creditably, but defeat didn't sit too well in some quarters. A number of fans were tearing Kezar apart.

Things were much quieter in the 49ers locker room. Players reflected on the season, and looked ahead. Some, like star linebacker Wilcox, had a rather wry view. "At this moment", Wilcox said, "I'm only thinking about that mile and three-quarters we have to run next July, when training camp opens".

For some, the memory of that first foray in 1971 has dimmed, even vanished. "I don't remember anything about it at all", 49ers cornerback Johnson said. Gene Washington, the 49ers wide receiver and future NFL executive, admitted he was short on specifics too. "But, I do remember the whole tone and excitement going into that game".

Nolan, who passed away in 2007, had come to terms with the defeat losing to his mentor, Landry, who is also gone. On that memorable day it was Dick Nolan against Tom Landry, almost like Tom Landry against Vince Lombardi. Landry couldn't get past Lombardi, and Nolan never could get past Landry in three playoff tries. At the end of that game, Nolan told his team they'd be back again, and they did. But in this game, the 49ers just didn't have enough experience to get over the hill.

-Dwight Chapin

10

The Players

'Playmakers' refers to 49ers players whose achievements for the team at Kezar Stadium altered history for the better. My list includes 49ers Hall of Fame members, All-Pro players, Pro-Bowlers and players whose exploits in a single season, or even a single game, have lived on through the years.

FRANKIE ALBERT

Quarterback, Punter, Coach 1946-1952
(1956-1958 Head Coach)

Albert was the master of the T-formation, and was ranked among the top five AAFC passers from 1946-49. He also made a strong contribution as a punter in both the AAFC and the NFL with an even 44.0 career average. That's amazing by today's standards.

A Kezar Moment

"October 9, 1949, I passed for 5 touchdowns to lead a 56-28 upset of the perennial AAFC world champion, the Cleveland Browns. That was my biggest day as a Niner".

199

KERMIT ALEXANDER

Defensive Back 1963-1969

Alexander was durable and missed only four of the 98 games with the 49ers. In 1965 alone, Alexander brought back 32 kickoffs, 35 punts for 1,003 yards, both NFL highs during that era.

A Kezar Moment

"My 41-yard punt return for a touchdown, and a 14-yard fumble recovery return for a touchdown in the 49ers 41-14 win over Chicago Bears, on December 11,1966".

JOE ARENAS

Offensive Back, Punt and
Kick Returner, 1951-1957

After a brilliant college career in football, basketball, baseball and track, Arenas became a splendid kick and punt returner with the 49ers. In 1953, he led the NFL in kickoff returns with a 34.4 average, and from 1954-57, Arenas led the 49ers in punt returns until retirement in 1958.

A Kezar Moment

"I have few of them. A 90-yard touchdown gallop against Detroit, and a 96-yarder versus the Colts in 1956, and a 82-yard dash punt return for a touchdown against the Eagles in 1953."

BRUNO BANDUCCI

Offensive Guard, Defensive Tackle
1946-1954

Banducci was favorite of the 49ers fans. He provided leadership in the trenches that helped spring the team's swift backfield of Joe Perry, Norm Standlee, John Strzykalski and Hugh McElhenny with his blocking.

A Kezar Moment

"Defensively, I enjoyed one of my biggest days on opening day, August 31, 1947, pressuring highly regarded Brooklyn Dodgers quarterback Glen Dobbs, sacking him twice and forcing two fumbles in a 23-7 49ers victory".

ALYN BEALS

Offensive End, Defensive End
1946-1951

Before Jerry Rice, there was Alyn Beals. He was the AAFC all-time leading scorer. Beals teamed with Frankie Albert to start a dynasty of 49ers' tradition of explosive offenses.

A Kezar Moment

"Scoring my first touchdown ever at Kezar in front of our fans. It was a pass from Albert against the Chicago Rockets on August 24, 1946".

REX BERRY

Defensive Back, Halfback
1951-1956

Nicknamed "The Carbon Comet," Berry immediately made contributions to the 49ers his rookie year, and helped enable the team to finish 7-4-1, 7-5 and 9-3 in his first three years on the team. Berry led the team in interceptions in 1953 and 1954.

A Kezar Moment

"On October 16, 1955, I made a 44-yard interception return for a touchdown against the Detroit Lions in a 27-24 win".

BRUCE BOSLEY

Offensive Guard, Center,
Defensive End 1956-1968

His toughness on the 49ers offensive line spanned the days of the "alley-oop", the shotgun offense and John Brodie's coming of age.

A Kezar Moment

"My moment of affirmation was on October 25, 1964, as I raced downfield to shake the hand of Vikings defensive end, Jim Marshall, after he had run 66 yards the wrong way with a recovered fumble to give the 49ers a safety".

JOHN BRODIE

Quarterback 1957-1973

He was a homegrown 49ers quarterback, as well as a professional golfer. He led the team to three consecutive playoff appearances in 1970, '71 and '72.

A Kezar Moment

"An 80-yard touchdown strike to Dave Parks against the Vikings on October 25, 1964. It was a thing of beauty".

TOMMY DAVIS

Kicker, Punter 1959-1969

Davis was a rare kicker who was equally adept at punting and kicking, making him particularly valuable to the team.

A Kezar Moment

"A 53-yard field against the Rams in a 45-21 win on October 17, 1965, and an 82-yard punt against the Vikings on September 30, 1962 in a 21-7 win".

BILL JOHNSON

Center, Linebacker 1948-1956

Nicknamed "Tiger," Johnson played at, or near the level of the best centers of his time. He selflessly anchored the offensive line clearing the way for the 49ers running attack, the best backfield in football from 1952-54.

A Kezar Moment

"Blocking for "The Million Dollar Backfield" of Y.A. Tittle, Hugh McElhenny, Joe Perry and John Henry Johnson, and helping Perry have back-to-back 1,000-yard seasons in 1953 and 1954".

JIMMY JOHNSON

Cornerback, Wide Receiver, Running back 1961-1976

He is recognized as one of the best man-for-man defenders in league history. Johnson had so great a reputation that opposing quarterbacks rarely threw in his direction. In Johnson's 16 year career with the 49ers, he had 47 interceptions, 2nd all-time 49ers record.

A Kezar Moment

"Playing receiver I made 11 receptions for 181 yards against the Detroit Lions on November 11, 1962".

CHARLIE KRUEGER

Defensive Tackle, Defensive End
1959-1973

A ferocious tackler, who always
had two or three opponents blocking
him in a game. He was recognized
as a quarterback dumping machine,
because of his numerous quarterback
sacks. In 1964 his teammates voted
him the Len Eshmont Award as the
49er who best exemplified courage
and inspiration.

A Kezar Moment

"Every game I played at Kezar, I
never wanted to get my butt whipped
out there. Not a chance".

HUGH McELHENNY

Halfback, Flanker, Kickoff and
Punt Returner 1952-1960

He was known as the "King" of
the running backs during his career
with the 49ers. McElhenny was the
master at open-field running with
sudden bursts of speed. He was a
member of the famed "Million Dollar
Backfield". Counting rushing,
receiving, kick-off and punt returns,
he totaled 11,369 yards.

A Kezar Moment

"The first time I touched the
football as a rookie, I ran 42 yards
to a touchdown in the 49ers 36-14
win against the Chicago Cardinals on
August 24, 1952".

205

LEO NOMELLINI

Defensive Tackle,
Offensive Tackle 1950-1963

Recognized by his teammates and opponents as "Leo the Lion", he made life miserable for opponents for 14 seasons in the NFL playing for the 49ers. He never missed a single game. Nomellini had everything needed to be an all-time great - size, speed, agility, aggressiveness and most important, dedication to the game.

A Kezar Moment

"I played in 86 straight league games at Kezar, not including pre-season games. It was a record I truly earned and respected".

JOE PERRY

Fullback 1948-1960 1963

Known for his blazing speed, he earned the nickname "The Jet" and rightfully so. As a member of the 49ers "Million Dollar Backfield", Perry became the first player in the NFL to rush for 1,000 yards in two consecutive seasons (1953 and 54). Perry ranks second on the list of the 49ers all-time rushing leaders with 7,344 yards.

A Kezar Moment

"Breaking Steve Van Buren's all-time rushing mark against the LA Rams on October 5, 1958".

LEN ROHDE

Offensive Tackle, Defensive End
1960-1974

Rhode was one of the best tackles to ever adorn a 49ers uniform. He was 6'4" with broad shoulders and gained legitimacy for his blocking skills. He was a winner of the 1974 Len Eshmont Award, and his career spanned over 15 years.

A Kezar Moment

"During our 1970 championship game season run, our offensive line allowed quarterback, John Brodie to get sacked only five times, and two or three of those sacks came on blitzes that weren't picked up by our backs".

BOB ST. CLAIR

Offensive and Defensive Tackle
1953-1963

At 6-foot 9-inches, St. Clair, nicknamed "The Geek" was the tallest tackle in the NFL. He intimidated many opponents with his size, speed, intelligence and a genuine love of hitting. He was extremely popular with fans and his teammates.

A Kezar Moment

"I was once kicked in the face while trying to block a punt by Hall of Fame quarterback Norm Van Brocklin. I made the play, but lost five teeth. I blocked 10 field goals playing goal-line defense in 1956".

GORDY SOLTAU

Offensive End, Kicker
1950-1958

Soltau led the NFL in scoring in 1953, and accounted for 644 points in his career. In the 49ers thrilling 44-17 win over the LA Rams at Kezar in 1951, he caught three touchdowns, and kicked a field goal and five extra points for a total of 26 points.

A Kezar Moment

"On October 4, 1953 against the Rams with five seconds left, I kicked a 12-yard field goal to cap a see-saw 31-30 victory. Another game against our archrival Rams, played on October 4, 1956, I booted four field goals in our 33-30 win".

NORM STANDLEE

Fullback, Linebacker
1946-1952

Called "Big Chief", Standlee was one of the original 49ers. He was a 6-foot 2-inch, 238-pound fullback, and considered big for that era. He drew comparisons to legends Bronco Nagurski and Jim Thorpe. He was a crowd favorite at Kezar, averaging 4.9 yards per carry. He also was a back-up punter and returned kicks.

A Kezar Moment

"Blocking for quarterback Frankie Albert. As teammates we used the same T-formation backfield during our glory years at Stanford under Clark Shaughnessy".

Y.A. TITTLE

Quarterback 1951-1960

As a member of the 49ers "Million Dollar Backfield", he guided one of the most potent offenses ever in the NFL. In nine impressive seasons with the 49ers, Tittle's claim to fame was developing the "alley-oop" pass play with R.C. Owens, a former basketball player, who out leaped defenders downfield for touchdowns.

A Kezar Moment

"Our come-from-behind win over the Detroit Lions on November 3, 1957. With just 11 ticks left to play, I tossed a 41-yard pass to a whirling, vertical Owens for another crazy-quilt 35-31 win".

GENE WASHINGTON

Wide Receiver 1969-1977

He had a sense for the ball, sure hands, and an instinctive rapport with quarterback John Brodie. The pair helped lead the 49ers to their first NFC Western Division title in 1970. During that season alone, the Brodie-to-Washington connection connected on 53 passes for 1,100 yards and 12 touchdowns.

A Kezar Moment

"One particular play I recall was a 35-yard toss from Brodie, where I made a one-handed catch for a touchdown to preserve a 24-20 win over the Atlanta Falcons on December 6, 1970".

DAVE WILCOX

Linebacker 1964-1974

Wilcox simply was the best linebacker the 49ers ever had, and they have had many. His long arms, speed and devastating tackling earned him All-Pro four times. Wilcox thrived on action and was compared to Dick Butkus for his tenacity.

A Kezar Moment

"My only NFL touchdown ... a 21-yard interception leading to a 35-21 win over the Falcons".

KEN WILLARD

Fullback 1965-1973

If you needed 2-yards, he was sure to get it for the team. To opposing defenses, the sight and impact of Willard slamming into the line was no joke. His consistency and durability helped the 49ers to three division playoffs (1970, '71 and '72).

A Kezar Moment

"The games blocking for quarterback John Brodie. Keeping him healthy was always my main concern".

BILLY WILSON

End-Flanker 1951-1960

Known as "Mr. Automatic", Wilson caught passes for the 49ers from Frankie Albert, much of the Y.A. Tittle's period with the 49ers and dawning of the John Brodie era. The sure-hander Wilson was the 49ers go-to receiver throughout the '50s decade. He was durable, missing only one game in a five-year span from 1953-57.

A Kezar Moment

"Yes, in the 1957 playoff game against Detroit I hauled in 9 passes for 107 yards and a touchdown".

ABE WOODSON

Defensive back, Kick Returner 1958-1964

Woodson was a playmaker. With his great speed, he demonstrated the ability to make a big play on the field. Although in college, he was a track and football star, he did not play halfback on the 49ers. As a kick returner, he led the NFL in 1959, 1962 and 1963.

A Kezar Moment

"On November 5, 1961, I made an 80-yard punt return to tie the Detroit Lions 20-20".

11

All-Decade Team

1946 - 1949

Offense	Defense
E – Alyn Beals	E – Gail Bruce
T – Bob Bryant	T – Don Carlin
G – Visco Grgich	T – Bruno Banducci
C – Bill Johnson	E – Don Clark
G – Bruno Banducci	LB – Pete Wiseman
T – Ron Woudenberg	LB – Visco Grgich
E – Hal Shoener	LB – Bob Bryant
QB – Frankie Albert	B – Jim Cason
B – John Strzykalski	B – Lowell Wagner
B – Len Eshmont	B – Eddie Carr
B – Norm Standlee	B – Sam Cathcart

K – Joe Vetrano   P – Frankie Albert

pictured: Len Eshmont

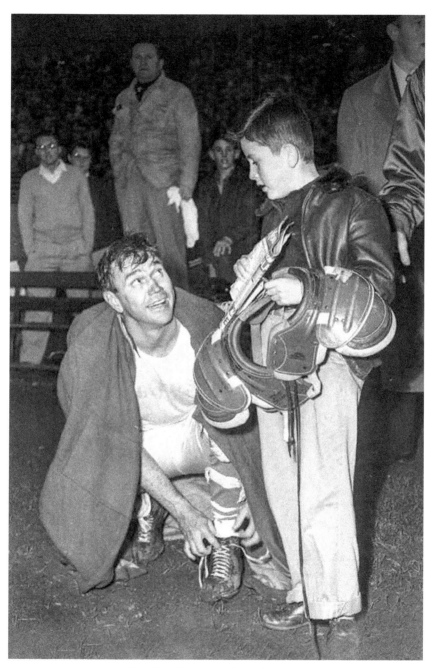

Frankie Albert after his final game

1950 - 1959

Offense	Defense
E – Gordy Soltau	DE – Charley Powell
T – Bob St. Clair	T – Leo Nomellini
G – Bruce Bosley	T – Clay Matthews
C – Frank Morze	DE – Ed Henke
G – Ted Connolly	LB – Matt Hazeltine
T – Bob Toneff	LB – Carl Rubke
E – Billy Wilson	LB – Hardy Brown
QB – Y.A. Tittle	DB – Rex Berry
HB – Hugh McElhenny	DB – Jim Ridlon
HB – Joe Perry	S – Jerry Mertens
F – R.C. Owens	S – Dicky Moegle
K – Gordy Soltau	P – Bill Jessup

pictured: Jerry Mertens

Dicky Moegle

1960 - 1970

Offense	Defense
E – Gene Washington	DE – Tommy Hart
T – Cas Banaszek	T – Charlie Krueger
G – Walt Rock	T – Monte Clark
C – Forrest Blue	DE – Dan Colchico
G – Howard Mudd	LB – Frank Nunley
T – Len Rhode	LB – Dave Wilcox
TE – Monty Stickles	LB – Skip Vanderbundt
QB – John Brodie	DB – Kermit Alexander
HB – J.D. Smith	DB – Jimmy Johnson
FB – Ken Willard	S – Dave Baker
F – Bernie Casey	S – Abe Woodson
K – Tommy Davis	P – Tommy Davis

pictured: Dave Baker

John Brodie receives his 1970 NFL Most Valuable Player award

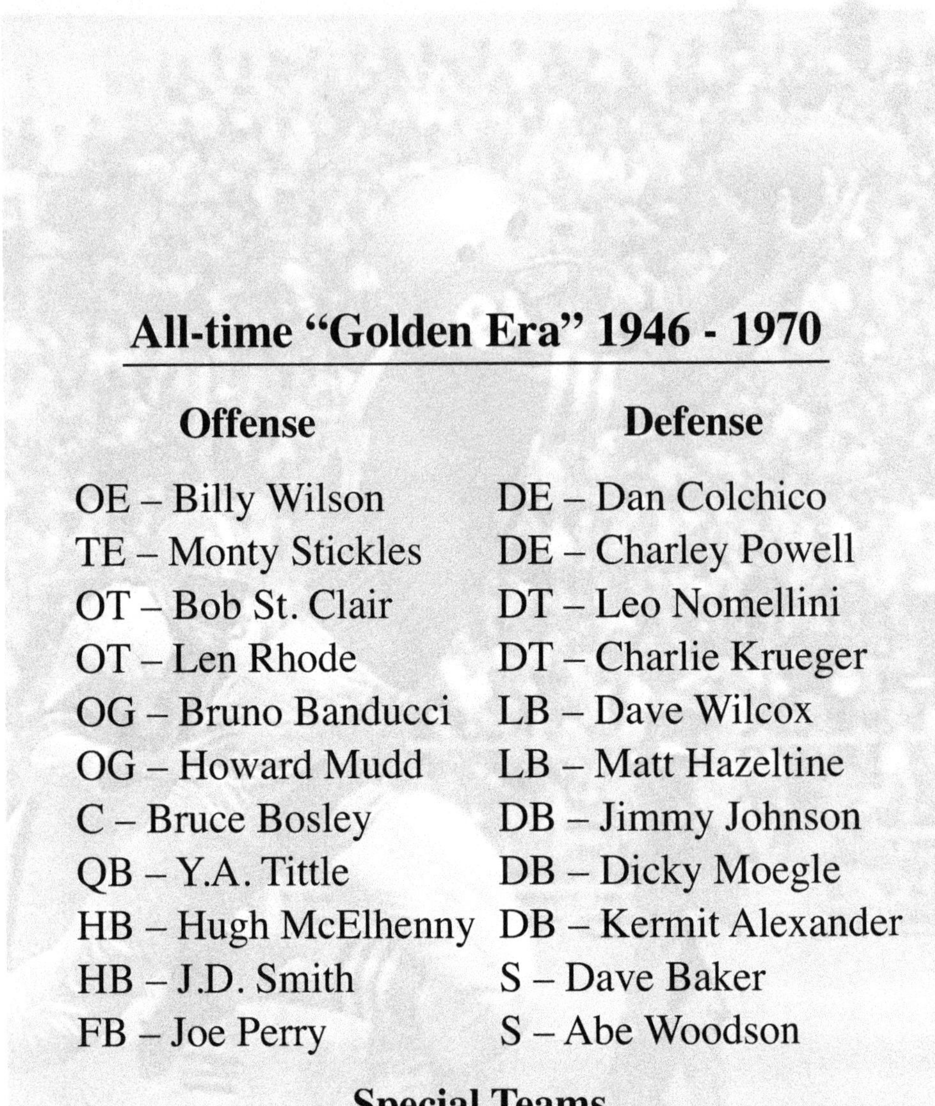

All-time "Golden Era" 1946 - 1970

Offense

OE – Billy Wilson
TE – Monty Stickles
OT – Bob St. Clair
OT – Len Rhode
OG – Bruno Banducci
OG – Howard Mudd
C – Bruce Bosley
QB – Y.A. Tittle
HB – Hugh McElhenny
HB – J.D. Smith
FB – Joe Perry

Defense

DE – Dan Colchico
DE – Charley Powell
DT – Leo Nomellini
DT – Charlie Krueger
LB – Dave Wilcox
LB – Matt Hazeltine
DB – Jimmy Johnson
DB – Dicky Moegle
DB – Kermit Alexander
S – Dave Baker
S – Abe Woodson

Special Teams

PR – Joe Arenas   KR – Abe Woodson
K – Tommy Davis   P – Tommy Davis

Head Coach

Lawrence "Buck" Shaw

pictured: Billy Wilson

Frankie Albert and "Buck" Shaw reunite at Kezar

12

Numbers and Statistics

These pages contain San Francisco 49ers records set during the team's 25-years at Kezar, plus relevant listings.

Longest Plays

Hugh McElhenny
82-yard touchdown run, vs Dallas Texans, October 26, 1952

John Brodie
80-yard touchdown pass to Dave Parks vs Minnesota Vikings October 25, 1964

Larry Barnes
86-yard punt, vs Chicago Cardinals, September 29, 1957

Hall of Famers

DT – **Leo Nomellini**
DT – **Bob St. Clair**
FB – **Joe Perry**
HB – **Hugh McElhenny**
HB – **John Henry Johnson**
QB – **Y.A. Tittle**
DB – **Jimmy Johnson**
LB – **Dave Wilcox**

Retired Numbers

12 – **John Brodie** QB
14 - **Y.A. Tittle** QB
34 – **Joe Perr**y RB
35 - **John Henry Johnson** HB
37 – **Jimmy Johnson** DB
39 – **Hugh McElhenny** HB
70 – **Charlie Krueger** DT
73 – **Leo Nomellini** OT
79 – **Bob St. Clair** OT

Players' Big Days

Rushing Yards
  Joe Perry 174 yards vs. Detroit Lions, November 2, 1958
Passing
  Y.A. Tittle 29 of 44, 371 yards vs. Baltimore Colts
  December 13, 1953
Touchdown Passes
  John Brodie 5 vs. Minnesota Vikings, November 28, 1965
Receiving
  Billy Wilson 8 receptions vs. Chicago Bears, November 9, 1952
Field Goals
  Gordy Soltau 4 vs. Los Angeles Rams, October 7, 1956

49ers Head Coaches

1946-54 **Lawrence "Buck" Shaw**
1955 **Norman "Red" Strader**
1956-58 **Frankie Albert**
1959-63 **Howard "Red" Hickey**
1963-67 **Jack Christensen**
1968-71 **Dick Nolan**

Years Played at Kezar

15 – **John Brodie** Quarterback, 1957-71
14 – **Matt Hazeltine** Linebacker, 1955-68
14 – **Leo Nomellini** Defensive Tackle, 1950-63
14 – **Joe Perry** Fullback, 1948-60, 1963
13 – **Charlie Krueger** Defensive Tackle, 1959-71
12 – **Bob St. Clair** Offensive Tackle, 1953-64
11 – **Jimmy Johnson** Defensive Back, 1961-71

Career Leaders

Passing
John Brodie 102 touchdowns, 13,850 yards
Rushing
Joe Perry 5,235 yards, 46 touchdowns
Receiving
Billy Wilson 202 receptions, 2,738 yards
26 touchdowns

Kezar Nemeses

George Halas Bears
Norm Van Brocklin Rams
Gino Marchetti Colts
Art Donovan Colts
Dick Butkus Bears
Alex Karras Lions
Harlon Hill Bears
Sam Huff Giants
Bill George Bears
Elroy Hirsch Rams
Raymond Berry Colts
Tobin Rote Lions
Les Richter Rams
Otto Graham Browns

500-Yard Games

597 vs. Colts, December 13, 1953
536 vs. Bears, November 19, 1961
534 vs. Redskins, September 29, 1954
521 vs. Rams, October 8, 1961
517 vs. Falcons, September 24, 1967

49ers Won, Lost, Tied
Regular Season Games

Green Bay Packers 13-5-1
Baltimore Colts 11-9
Los Angeles Rams 10-10-1
Detroit Lions 10-9-1
Chicago Bears 10-8
New York Yankees 4-3
Los Angeles Dons 4-0
Cleveland Browns 3-5-1
Chicago Rockets 3-0
Washington Redskins 3-0-1
Atlanta Falcons 3-1
Philadelphia Eagles 3-1
Pittsburgh Steelers 3-1
Minnesota Vikings 2-4-1
Dallas Cowboys 2-1
Buffalo Bills 2-0-1
Chicago Cardinals 1-3
Denver Broncos 1-0
Chicago Hornets 1-0
Buffalo Bisons 1-0
New Orleans Saints 1-0-1
Miami Seahawks 1-0
Dallas Texans 1-0
New York Giants 0-2

Best in the West

Dick Nolan took over a moribund 49ers team in 1968. He led them to their greatest success, and helmed three consecutive Western Division Champions (1970, 1971 and 1972)

All-Time NFL Records

Team with fewest fumbles:
4, 1960 49ers

Most consecutive seasons scoring safety:
3, Charlie Krueger 1959-1961

Most seasons leading league in kickoff returns:
3, Abe Woodson, 1959, 1962–63

First player with 1,200 career pass completions:
Y.A. Tittle, 1952-60

Best Playoff Games

Passing
John Brodie 19/40, 262 yards, 1 touchdown
vs Dallas Cowboys, January 3, 1971

Rushing
Frankie Albert 9/51 yards, 8/17, 96 yards passing,
1 touchdown vs New York Yankees, December 4, 1949

Receiving
Billy Wilson 9/107 yards, 1 touchdown, vs Detroit Lions
December 22, 1957

Kezar Snapshots

Hugh McElhenny, Joe Perry and Leo Nomellini are honored having their numbers retired

Dave Parks and George Mira accommodate young fans with their autographs

Quarterbacks Frankie Albert, Y.A Tittle and Jim Powers

Y.A. Tittle, Clyde Conner and Billy Wilson admire Bob St. Clair's new automobile

John Brodie and Frank Morze entertain youngsters on 49ers Camera Day

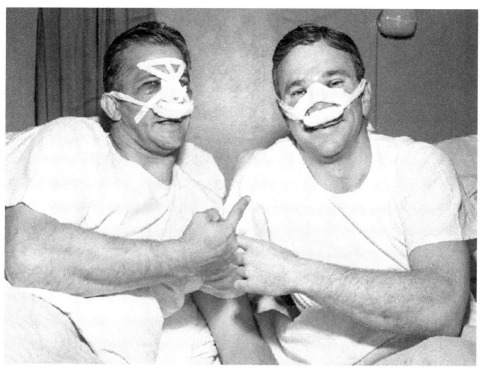

Johnny Strzykalski and Frankie Albert point fingers, while enduring nose rehab

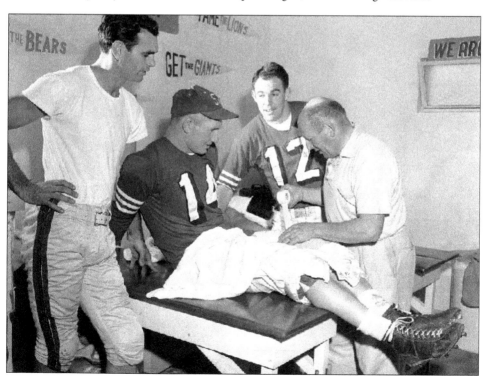

Billy Wilson and John Brodie watch, while Y.A. Tittle has his leg taped by trainer Henry Schmidt

Dave Parks

Matt Hazeltine

Ken Willard

Bernie Casey

Elbert Kimbrough and Kermit Alexander relax, awaiting their turn to re-enter the game

R.C. Owens is surrounded by adoring fans on Camera Day

A true 49ers fan, singer Tony Bennett entertains the Kezar audience

Clyde Conner shows-off his muscle for the cameras

BOOTH 3A

12 NOON SATURDAY, DEC. 21

TICKETS SOLD TO HOLDERS OF FORTY NINER CERTIFICATES ONLY

GENERAL ADMISSION TICKETS
WILL GO ON SALE AT
BOX OFFICE 20
OPPOSITE POLY HIGH

12 NOON SATURDAY
LIMIT 4

20

49ers fan, first in line for tickets, is greeted by a friendly police horse

Acknowledgements

I wish to extend my sincere appreciation to the hundreds of 49ers fans, players, coaches and media, who provided their recollections and experiences - on and off the field - during memorable moments at Kezar Stadium. Special thank you to all, including Dennis Caracciolo for his article "The 49ers replay - The Heartbreak of 1957", published in the *San Jose Mercury News* in 2007; Christopher Pollack, Historian for the San Francisco Recreation and Park Department; Bob Zingmark, my editor and layout man, whose experience and knowledge enabled me to ascertain information, and verify many facts and statistics in this project.

Thanks to Ed Cooper, Henry Michalski, Barry Tomkins, Joe Fonzi and Sue Brodie, who rallied around my project with enthusiasm and gracious support; the San Francisco 49ers staff - past and present - starting with former Media Public Relations Director, Jerry Walker, a man whose knowledge knows no end; Bill Van Niekerken, Library Editor for the *San Francisco Chronicle*; Northern California Alumni NFL Chapter; San Francisco 49ers archives; The Western Neighborhood Project Foundation.

Also, to the 49ers fan members on internet websites: Official San Francisco 49ers message board • 49ers Webzone • 49ers Fan Zone • Niner Empire Faithful • 49ers Dynasty • Red and Gold Forever • 49ers

Faithful for Life • Forever Faithful Illinois • Colorado 49ers Fans • Niner Empire Great Britain • Scottish 49ers Chapter.

Special thanks to Frank Rippon and Bill Fox, 49ers photographers, for their amazing images of Kezar, and memories of the stadium; Greg Garr, who graciously provided photographs from his personal collection; Cal-Pictures archival resources, Associated Press and United Press International, and Getty images.

To the authors and writers, Dr. Kristine Setting Clark *St. Clair, I'll Take It Raw!*, and *Nothing Comes Easy: My Life in Football: Y.A. Tittle*; Dan McGuire *San Francisco 49ers*; Dennis Georgatos *Stadium Stories*; John Brodie *Open Field*; Matt Maiocco *San Francisco 49ers: Where have You Gone?*; Dennis Georgatos *Game of Life: The San Francisco 49ers*; Bob Carroll, David Neff, Michael Gershman and John Thorn *Total 49ers*; Dave Newhouse *Founding 49ers*; Daniel Brown *100 Things 49ers Fans Should Know & Do Before They Die*; Mickey Herskowitz *The Golden Age of Pro Football*; Harvey Aronson *Pro Football's Most Passionate Fans*; New York Times *The History of the San Francisco 49ers*; Los Angeles Times *A Football History:-San Francisco 49ers*; and to Carl Nolte, Dwight Chapin, Scott Ostler, Bill Leiser of the *San Francisco Chronicle* for their assistance in their newspaper columns; Bob Brachman, Glen Dickey, *San Francisco Examiner*; Rich Mueller, *Sports Collectors Daily*; and Bob Swick, *Gridiron Greats*.

Lastly, I'd like to give special thanks to the large group of San Francisco 49ers fans featured in this book, who took the time and made the effort which helped make this book possible. I can't thank you enough for your contributions. *Kezar Stadium- 49ers Fans Remember* is my greatest accomplishment, and I'm pleased it has come to fruition.

Meet the Author

As a writer and collector of 49ers memorabilia for over six decades, Martin S. Jacobs has established himself in virtually all aspects of the team's 75-year history. His journey began as a youth in the 1950s vending at old Kezar Stadium. During the tumultuous 1970s and into the Super '80s, he operated the "Sports Stop," serving the 49ers Faithful with team apparel, souvenirs and collectibles. In 2000, Jacobs was bestowed with the honor of being selected the '49ers No. 1 Fan of the Year by VISA International.' A plaque of commendation for the 49ers is on display at the NFL Hall of Fame.

In a span of 50 years, he has covered the 49ers for *Pro Football Weekly, Football Digest, The Sporting News, Street & Smith's NFL annuals, Gridiron Greats,* and as "The Collector" in the 49ers *Gameday* magazine. He has authored three other books with 49ers historical significance: *Before They Were Champions - the San Francisco 49ers 1958 Season; San Francisco 49ers - Images of Sport;* and S*an Francisco 49ers Legends-The Golden Age of Pro Football.* Also, in 2015, Jacobs was featured by 49ers Studio films in their weekly 49ers' Faithful TV series (No. 7), as the "Throwback." Today Jacobs resides in San Francisco with his family. He welcomes your comments and can be reached by email at MJacobs784@aol.com.

A Tribute to 49ers Legends

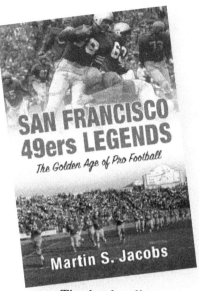

Available from author Martin Jacobs is *San Francisco 49ers LEGENDS-The Golden Age of Pro Football.* This book is a complement to *Kezar Stadium -49ers Fans Remember,* and definitive story of the 49ers football team beginning from their swirling tales in the All-American Football Conference, to playing in the NFL. The book tells a story about the 49ers players we read about in newspapers, listened to on play-by-play radio broadcasts and eventually watched on television - Frankie Albert, Norm Standlee, Joe Perry, Y.A. Tittle, Hugh McElhenny, R.C. Owens, Leo Nomellini, Bob St. Clair, John Brodie and so many others. The book is a true narrative account encapsulating the deeds and foibles of the 49ers players who, by performance, personality or both, gave flavor and substance to those times. 49ers fans will find this book, not just the story of a football team coming of age, but a stirring, evocative collection of reminiscences touching upon what it means to be a 49ers fan. If you loved *Kezar Stadium-49ers Fans Remember,* you will love this book.

The softbound 6" x 9" book totals 305-pages, with an array of 50 publicity and action photographs. There are 49 chapters with personal interviews, and a chapter devoted to investing in 49ers relics and memorabilia. The book is available at amazon.com for $22.50 plus $3.50 shipping, or $9.95 (Kindle version). A signed copy is available emailing the author Martin Jacobs at MJacobs784@aol.com. Personal checks and money orders accepted by writing: P.O. Box 22026, San Francisco, CA 94122. Paypal accepted using author's email address.

Goodbye Kezar...
Thanks for the Memories!

CPSIA information can be obtained
at www.ICGtesting.com
Printed in the USA
BVHW041825100121
597498BV00031B/533